Alastair Little's Italian Kitchen

Alastair Little's Italian Kitchen

Recipes from La Cacciata

Photography by James Merrell

Ebury Press
LONDON

Author's Acknowledgements

With many thanks to Fran Fullenwider for putting up with me and to Sarah Robson for helping me assemble the recipes from La Cacciata.

First published in 1996

1 3 5 7 9 10 8 6 4 2

Text copyright © Alastair Little 1996
Photography copyright © James Merrell 1996

First published in the United Kingdom in 1996 by Ebury Press
Random House, 20 Vauxhall Bridge Road, London SW1V 2SA

Random House Australia (Pty) Limited
20 Alfred Street, Milsons Point, Sydney, New South Wales 2061, Australia

Random House New Zealand Limited
18 Poland Road, Glenfield, Auckland 10, New Zealand

Random House South Africa (Pty) Limited
PO Box 337, Bergvlei, South Africa

Random House UK Limited Reg. No. 954009

A catalogue record for this book is available from the British Library.

ISBN 0 09 181365 4

Editor Susan Fleming

Design Senate
Photography James Merrell

Food styling Louise Pickford
Styling Roisin Nield

Colour reproduction by Resolve Consultancy
Printed and bound in Portugal by Printer Portuguesa L.d.a.

contents

Introduction

There is no real Italian food outside of Italy. Sure, there is trendy Italianate food, at best a delicious pastiche, and there are occasional flashes of brilliance from neighbourhood Marios or Francos, but on the whole the thing has become a bit of a performance, a production of fashion and wishful thinking. In Italy it all happens rather more easily; good food, be it at home or in restaurants, is an everyday occurrence: commonplace, familiar and, exactly as expected, delicious. This cooking is done with whatever produce is seasonally available to a repertoire of orally transmitted recipes, largely of local origin. The importance of this locality cannot be stressed enough. It is almost fatuous to discuss Italian food as a whole when you bear in mind that the country is still imperfectly unified, and anything from another region is always referred to as *straniero*, foreign. The only common denominator between the various regional kitchens is a fondness for pasta.

In restaurants the best food is often the cheapest. You would be wise to ignore the menu, particularly if it is translated into four languages, and accept the waiter's advice. Indeed he may wish to settle your pasta order before you have sat down. The posher the restaurant the more the simplicity of the food disappears, except in a few exalted cases where the concept of elegant restraint is carried to extremes. Less definitely becomes more when you get your bill.

Italians wouldn't dream of buying food in supermarkets - they use them for toothpaste, nappies and bleach, that's about it. Markets thrive, speciality shops still prosper, and their customers await with relish the seasonal arrival of locally produced food, the canon of fruit and vegetables from spring to summer, unfolding into autumn with game, mushrooms and truffles then rounding off in winter with the new pulses and olive oil. You can be certain that everybody knows exactly what to do with this stuff as it arrives.

All this didn't dawn on me until I first arrived to work in Orvieto five years ago clutching an armful of carefully researched recipes - then quickly found I couldn't do any of them. The food I'd chosen was either out of season or simply unavailable in that region. No choice but to come round to their way of thinking: shopping first, then much discussion about what to do with it and finally a blazing row about precisely whose mother's recipe to follow. This approach seemed to me to be sensible - a balanced way of approaching cooking and eating. Suddenly things seemed so much simpler, and I wonder if this is due to an innate Italian talent or a national indolence.

The strictures of seasonality, locality and simplicity in no way limit the scope of the cook; on the contrary, they are immensely liberating. Even the poorest region will have an enormous range of dishes to choose from. Asparagus, peas, broad beans and artichokes are the only vegetables good in May, but who could get bored cooking or eating an endless succession of pasta, antipasti, risotti, minestre and frittate incorporating them. They are enjoyed and then other produce replaces them until next year. To elaborate or embellish these dishes will ruin them; inventive cooks are not welcome here.

This is not a Utopian view. One can and frequently does eat badly in Italy, but that is due to sloppy cooking and most often found in areas over-infested with tourists. On a day-to-day basis the Italians eat better than any nation I know. The underlying bone structure of the food is so fabulous that misapplied cosmetic touches or familiarity cannot completely mask it. Prosaic excellence is the quality that has entranced me for twenty years, and what this book hopes to communicate.

La Cacciata

The name sounds as though it might have been something to do with hunting, but apparently it means 'refuge' in an archaic dialect and refers to a post-battle rescue of survivors from a Visigothic invasion in the fifth century AD. The estate is perched atop a conical hill of volcanic origin, itself on top of the high craggy ridge facing Orvieto from the south. La Cacciata has been in continuous habitation for 2,500 years. The Etruscans began the construction of the extensive galleries under the hill, probably as tombs, but they now serve as the wine cellars. The present owners, the Belcapo family, have only been there for the last 200 years.

The view of Orvieto across the valley, with its umber walls and the unbelievable magnificence of the Duomo, is simply stunning. Turner stayed there on his way to Rome and painted his version of the view, which now hangs in the Tate. The nature of Umbrian light has been an artistic cliché through the centuries, but it is in no way exaggerated, changing both subtly and dramatically every day.

The estate buildings at La Cacciata are not splendid, the main villa appearing dilapidated to tidier North European perceptions. The oil mill, farmhouse and cottages are all rather rustic and basic, but this is a working farm, combining three main functions: the production of excellent olive oil, a range of Orvieto Classico wines and a bed and breakfast business. It is the facilities of the last that Sarah Robson and I rent to house our cooking school. The guest rooms are in the former labourers' cottages and are very simple indeed, particularly the plumbing. There are no formal gardens, just dusty pathways through the vines. This is not a 'Chiantishire' Disneyland.

The food taught and served at La Cacciata matches the location, being essentially rustic, very seasonal, often home grown or bought at market. Herbs grow extravagantly everywhere; rosemary and fennel are almost omnipresent in the local meat cookery. The estate's fruit trees provide desserts, wild mushrooms flourish in autumn, and truffles are available cheaply and in abundance from the local truffle master and his charming dogs. The farmhouse kitchen has a large stone bread oven outside which is used regularly, and all grilling is done on a primitive but effective barbecue. All this is the antithesis of high-tech cookery but the food is so natural and simple that this is the perfect environment to prepare and eat it in.

Alastair Little, May 1996

A Note on Olive Oil

A unifying theme of any food at La Cacciata is the excellent oil produced on the estate. However, we do not use this olive oil all the time. It is far too good to fry with or to use where strong flavours – garlic, chilli, anchovy

etc – are present. Here are my three grades of olive oils as used throughout this book. (The quantities given in the recipes are not absolutely precise – you can generally vary them according to taste.)

Good Regular supermarket own brands or generic Italian brands of extra virgin olive oil are what I mean by good oil. They shouldn't be too expensive. These oils often come in large tins, which can be dramatically cheaper. So, if you intend to plough through this book, I advise you to buy a 4 litre tin!

Very good This category is a little vague, but covers oils that come from a single origin, are of course extra virgin, but do not belong to the top flight. Probably the best guide for this is price. I notice that several of the supermarkets stock quite a few oils in this range. Experiment until you find one you like. It does not come in tins, but is usually bottled at source.

Top-quality Here we are talking of single producer Tuscan and Umbrian oils, some of them offered in fancy packaging or bottles worthy of a perfumier and often not much cheaper. I sometimes wonder whether these oils are meant to be put on food or behind your ears. I only ever use these oils as a flavouring or enhancement on a suitable finished dish. Their effects can be miraculous on, for example, a dish of plainly boiled spinach or French beans. Perhaps, to show your guests how munificent you are, you should put the bottle on the table to let them add their own oil to the food.

■ Olive oil does not like sunlight, so store unopened in a cupboard and, when open, in your fridge. Otherwise it will spoil quite quickly. However, the better oils tend to set to a green sludge in the fridge, so warm to room temperature in plenty of time.

A Note on Equipment

There are three pieces of equipment that seem to be continually mentioned in the recipes in this book. One is a spider, another is cooking tongs and the third is a ridged cast-iron grill pan.

The spider is an open wire scoop with a long handle, used for retrieving items from boiling liquid or fat. In my experience the best ones are available in Chinese supermarkets and consist of a bamboo handle with something that resembles a flattened pan scourer at the end. They do the job much more efficiently than the European equivalent, or, what is often suggested, a slotted spoon. They are cheap, but not particularly durable.

Over the last five years, an American version of cooking tongs has spread throughout professional kitchens. They are springy, come in various lengths, and have a scalloped spoon at the end of each arm. They are made in Taiwan, and are incredibly cheap. Catering suppliers fail to stock them at their peril. They are simply the best thing for serving pasta, as they allow you to lift out individual portions of pasta and plonk them on a plate. Have you ever had to serve six plates of spaghetti and then resorted to scissors on particularly recalcitrant strands? The longer-handled versions are essential for barbecues. Incidentally, these were unknown in Italy until I introduced them, as were pizza wheels . . .

Dry-grilling on a ridged cast-iron grill pan is a healthy way of cooking. It is useful for steaks, other meats, fish and vegetables. The pan is heated until very hot, and the food is cooked directly on the hot surface, the ridges imprinting the food with dark stripes.

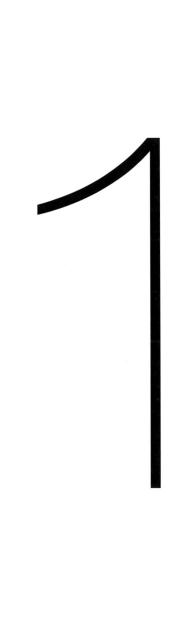

Antipasti

First Courses The name indicates that these are types of dishes that would precede pasta. This may have been true in the days of five- or six-course meals, but they are now generally served as an alternative to pasta. Most restaurants in Italy will display them for the customers to select for themselves. They vary between dried-out remnants to brilliantly colourful and appetising selections of wonderful dishes.

ANTIPASTI DI VERDURA
VEGETABLE FIRST COURSES

Italy must be a paradise for vegetarians. The number of recipes detailed below is only the tip of an iceberg. Every notable book on Italian cooking will have many others to offer. Anna del Conte's *Secrets from an Italian Kitchen* is one that I have used extensively over the years.

All these vegetable antipasti will feed between four and ten people, depending on the number of other dishes served.

ASPARAGI | ASPARAGUS

The most important thing about asparagus is freshness: size doesn't matter (don't you believe it, boys!), but uniformity of thickness does. Look for a high proportion of green sprout over white woody stem. English asparagus is generally very good, but often the paper wrapper covers an unacceptable amount of white wood, so pull one stalk out of the bunch to check (thereby incurring your local market trader's wrath). Very large asparagus are too expensive, but very thin 'sprue grass' can be delicious. Watch out for damaged, slightly wet, tips, and withered corrugated stems, as both of these indicate age.

All asparagus needs peeling, with the exception of sprue. The woody white bits need trimming, but keep all trimmings and peelings for making a stock base for asparagus risotto (see page 111). Asparagus grows in sandy soil, and will always need a wash.

Asparagi alla Griglia
Grilled Asparagus

Allow at least 6 stalks of medium asparagus per person; more, much more, would be appreciated. Peel, trim and wash. Season lightly.

Either barbecue or cook on a hot ridged grill pan for 5 minutes without moving, then turn and give the other side 5 minutes. It should be well marked and slightly wilted.

Remove with tongs to a serving dish and dress with a little top-quality olive oil and possibly some shaved Parmesan.

Asparagi Arrosti
Roast Asparagus

This is a surprisingly delicious method of cooking 'grass', but beware, it shrinks alarmingly in the oven. You will need a large roasting tray so the stalks can be laid out in a single layer.

Per person
10 medium asparagus stalks
salt and pepper
1 tbsp good olive oil
1/2 tsp balsamic vinegar or
    lemon juice

Preheat the oven to its maximum.

Peel, trim and wash the asparagus, then arrange in a roasting tray. Season, drizzle with oil and roast for 20 minutes. It will shrivel. Try one stalk for doneness; it should be very tender, the colour faded, but the flavour wonderfully concentrated. Remove to a serving dish and sprinkle with balsamic vinegar or lemon juice.

Asparagi Bolliti
Boiled Asparagus

A classic way of cooking asparagus, which is good hot, warm or at room temperature.

Per person
6 medium asparagus stalks
25 g butter
salt and pepper

Put a large deep pan of water on to boil. Peel, trim and wash the asparagus. Pack the asparagus into your pasta basket or equivalent. Salt the water, and plunge the asparagus into it when rapidly boiling. Cook for approximately 5 minutes. Melt the butter and put in a ramekin or suitable dish per person. Drain the asparagus, serve with the melted butter as a dip, and possibly lemon.

If you want to serve the asparagus cold, drain the stalks and dip them for 1 minute in cold water, then drain very thoroughly. Set aside until needed, do not refrigerate.

CARCIOFI | ARTICHOKES

Until recently, it was nonsense to discuss Italian artichoke recipes in Britain because one simply couldn't find the correct baby artichokes, and if you could, they were so old that they had developed a spiky choke. Now the real article can be found, so the following recipes may be attempted. The first one – Carciofi alla Romana – is in a way the master recipe because it is a reasonably foolproof method and details how to prepare the little blighters.

Carciofi alla Romana
Roman Artichokes

Traditionally prepared with catnip, but mint will do fine (and you'll avoid the attentions of stray moggies). Select artichokes with stems, and with heads of between 3 and 8 cm long. The leaves should be pliable and not too spiky. The preparation of artichokes may seem very complicated, but once you have seen it done, or had a go yourself, you'll understand the basics, and can be confident.

6 people
24 prepared baby artichokes
   (see method)
at least 6 lemons
1 large carrot, peeled,
   topped and tailed
1 celery stalk, strings removed
   (use a potato peeler)
1 medium white onion, peeled
200 ml very good olive oil
1/2 bottle dry white wine
2 bay leaves, 1 sprig marjoram,
   1 large sprig mint, tied
   into a bouquet garni

Little **Tips**

- Raw artichokes leave a metallic taint and colour on your hands, knife and chopping board when you are preparing them. Scrub off thoroughly.

- To make artichoke salad, drain Carciofi alla Romana. Quarter the artichokes, season and scatter with chopped parsley, a squeeze of lemon juice and some very good olive oil. Serve cold.

To prepare the artichokes, you will need lots of lemons and a large bowl of water into which you squeeze some of them. You will need a small serrated knife, a peeler and a small curved chef's knife usually known as a 'turning' knife.

Cut the stem 1 cm below the artichoke head and rub with the cut lemon. Cut the artichoke head itself halfway down from the top – be ruthless! – then discard the top and rub the cut surface with the cut lemon. Pull off the outer two or three layers of leaves until you expose pale tender leaves; rub these with lemon too. With the curved knife trim off the stubs of the leaves; rub these with lemon. Peel the stem with the peeler, then rub with lemon and put the artichoke in the lemon-acidulated water. Note the mantra 'rub with lemon'. Repeat with all the artichokes. As the cut lemon halves are used up, throw them into the water. The prepared artichokes can be stored completely covered in their water for up to a day in the fridge.

Cut the carrot, celery and onion into 5 mm dice.

Put the oil, wine, vegetables and herbs into a stainless-steel or enamelled pan, then add the artichokes, some salt and several whole peppercorns. Add 2 of the half lemons from the artichoke preparation. Add enough water to just cover the contents. Cover with greaseproof paper then insert a plate that will fit snugly inside the pan to hold down the artichokes, i.e. to keep them submerged (a smaller pan lid is very effective for this, and is known as a drop lid).

Bring to the boil over a high heat. Turn down the heat and simmer slowly for 10 minutes (if the artichokes are large, 15 minutes). Remove from the heat and allow to cool and finish cooking in their liquor. Transfer to a sealable container, preferably non-metallic, and store in the fridge until needed.

Carciofi alla Griglia
Grilled Artichokes

Both methods for this are based on Carciofi alla Romana. Serve hot, warm or at room temperature.

1 From raw Prepare the artichokes as for alla Romana, but do not cook them. Cut the artichokes in half longitudinally and grill for 10 minutes on the cut face, then 5 minutes on the round outer surfaces. Season whilst cooking, with salt and pepper, then dress with top-quality olive oil.

2 From cooked Assuming you have some cooked Carciofi alla Romana, drain, cut in half, season and grill over a fierce heat on the cut surface.

Carciofi Ripieni
Stuffed Artichokes

This is the dish to do if you can't find baby artichokes. Look for globe artichokes with stems as these form part of the stuffing. The preparation of globe artichokes for this dish is exactly the same as for baby artichokes; 'rub with lemon' is as important, but when you slice the top off you will expose the choke. This you must scrape out with a teaspoon or melon baller, and then you must remember to squeeze lemon into the cavity. Be ruthless with the outer leaves, as you must get down to the tender ones. Peel the stalk and trim leaf stubs as normal and remember, plenty of lemon. Keep in lemon-acidulated water until needed.

4 globe artichokes (1 per person),
    prepared as overleaf
good olive oil
1 large white onion,
    peeled and very finely diced
2 garlic cloves, peeled and minced
a large handful of fresh
    parsley, chopped
a little fresh oregano, chopped
250 g fresh breadcrumbs
salt and pepper
juice of 1 lemon

You will need a roasting dish with 4 cm sides which will compactly hold the artichokes in a single layer.

To prepare the stuffing, remove the stems from the artichokes, leaving a flat base on which the vegetables can sit stably. Dice the stems finely. Heat 2 tbsp olive oil in a frying pan over a medium heat. Add the artichoke stems and the onion, and sweat until tender and translucent, about 10 minutes. Add the garlic, parsley and oregano, then transfer to a bowl and mix with the breadcrumbs. The mixture should be just moist enough – because of the oil – to form a slightly cohesive paste when squeezed. If necessary add more oil. Season with salt and pepper and add some lemon juice.

Preheat the oven to 160–180°C/325–350°F/Gas 3–4. Spread open the centre of each artichoke and carefully spoon the stuffing into the cavities. Lightly oil the roasting dish and put the artichokes in, top side up. Pour 5 mm water into the dish, and sprinkle the artichokes with more oil and some salt and pepper, and put in the oven. The water will help prevent the artichokes sticking, and will hasten the cooking by generating steam, but as it may evaporate before they are done, watch carefully and add a little more if needed. They will take about 50 minutes, and the idea is that the water has disappeared about 5 minutes before they are done.

Allow to cool either partially or wholly, and serve with lemon wedges and (optional) good oil.

Carciofi alla Giudea
Jewish Artichokes

These 'Jewish' artichokes are a Roman speciality, which are served in the Ghetto, an ancient quarter of Rome. This is the oldest surviving native cuisine in Rome, and the best, and was introduced to me by Jonathan Meades, *The Times'* restaurant critic. The artichokes are deep-fried, like crisps on the outside but tender-hearted inside, and you eat everything. They must be very well drained otherwise they are greasy. They are an essential part of the Roman *fritto misto*, much beloved of Jonathan. This has nothing to do with deep-fried fish, and everything to do with the obscurer parts of a lamb (spleen, testicles, brain, spinal cord etc.). It is usually astonishingly good, with the unpleasant-looking but delicious parts being safely hidden in batter.

2–3 medium or small artichokes per person, 6–8 cm deep and wide (don't attempt to cater for more than 3 people)
2 lemons
1 litre sunflower oil

Trim the artichokes as on page 14, remove choke carefully, then store the artichokes in lemon-acidulated water. Before cooking, drain and dry thoroughly. Trim the stalks to 1 cm.

Heat the oil to 180°C/350°F and preheat the oven to 120°C/250°F/Gas 1/2.

You can cook 2 or 3 artichokes at a time, or the number the pan will hold in a single layer. Plunge them into the hot oil and then, with tongs, push each artichoke, leaves side down, firmly against the bottom of the pan in turn. Hold for 1 minute and repeat with the other artichokes in the oil. This pushing down will spread the leaves out and allow the oil to penetrate and crisp them separately.

After this initial blast, the artichokes will need a further 8–10 minutes. You may need to turn the heat down to medium. Occasionally turn and press them. When they are golden brown and very crisp, remove to a roasting tray with a rack in it to drain. Keep warm in the low oven until the remaining artichokes are cooked.

BIETOLE | SWISS CHARD

Bietole is the Italian word for the green leaf of Swiss chard. Spinach is generally unavailable in Orvieto in spring and summer, so this is used in its place. It has a similar taste, but a rather more robust texture, and is normally used in ravioli stuffings, crespelle and gnocchi.

It arrives with large white stalks, which are trimmed off and put on the compost heap. I know there are numerous recipes for these stalks, but I have tried most of them and come to the conclusion that it is cheaper to bin them raw. Their taste when prepared and cooked redefines the word 'uninteresting'.

Choose leaves that are not too pockmarked, and try to get a good ratio of leaf to stem. Wash well.

Insalata di Bietole Cotte
Cooked Swiss Chard Salad

1.5 kg Swiss chard,
    trimmed of stalks
salt and pepper
juice of 1 lemon
top-quality olive oil

Bring 4 litres salted water to the boil. Plunge the Swiss chard leaves in and blanch for 3–4 minutes. Drain and refresh briefly in cold water. Drain thoroughly, pressing lightly and repeatedly. Separate leaves and drain again. Arrange in a mound on a serving dish and grate a little nutmeg on, then add some salt and pepper, lemon juice and olive oil. Toss, and serve with more olive oil.

PEPERONI | PEPPERS

Peppers are one of the fundamental building blocks of Italian cuisine, particularly in the south. Red and yellow peppers are sweet members of the capsicum family. Do not use green peppers.

Peperoni Ripieni
Stuffed Peppers

One of these stuffed pepper ideas is adapted from the Blessed Elizabeth of David. The other is the invention of brilliant cook/writer Richard Whittington.

4 people
good olive oil
4 garlic cloves, peeled
    and finely sliced
salt and pepper

Whittington Peppers
2 medium red peppers
225 g buffalo mozzarella
8 good quality anchovy
    fillets, drained

Preheat the oven to 180°C/350°F/Gas 4.

Cut all the peppers in half longitudinally, carefully cutting the stem so half of it remains with each half pepper. Remove all the seeds and carefully pare away any white pith. Lightly oil two small oven trays (Swiss roll tins are ideal), and arrange the red peppers on one and the yellow on the other, bowl side up. Put two slices of garlic in each pepper, lightly drizzle with oil and season.

Put 1 tsp of pesto in each yellow pepper (or 2 or 3 torn basil leaves). Put 1 tomato in each yellow pepper. Carefully pour approximately 1/2 wine glass of water

Piedmontese Peppers

2 medium yellow peppers
4 tsp pesto or basil leaves
4 medium plum tomatoes, skinned

into the tray around the yellow peppers and put in the preheated oven. Add water to the red peppers, and put them in the oven as well.

Cook the peppers for 20 minutes, then brush the edges and stems with olive oil and return to the oven for a further 20 minutes. The water should have evaporated and the peppers will be beginning to fry in surplus oil in the trays. They should be slightly collapsed and charred on the edges. If not, give them 5 minutes more.

Set the Piedmontese peppers aside, and leave to cool at this point. Turn the oven up to 220°C/425°F/Gas 7. Slice the mozzarella and arrange in the red peppers. Criss-cross 2 anchovies on each and return to the oven, about 3–5 minutes.

Arrange the warm Piedmontese peppers and the hot Whittingtons on the individual plates (one of each colour). Scrape and spoon any pan juices over the respective peppers and serve with good bread.

Little **Tip**

■ Expert cooks of this dish become obsessed with generating copious quantities of slightly caramelised pepper juices mixed with olive oil. Over-oiling of this dish will spoil it.

Clockwise from top: Melanzane alla Griglia, Carciofi alla Romana, Peperoni Ripieni, Funghi alla Griglia, Asparagi Arrosti, Fagiolini con Aceto Balsamico e Olio di Tartufo.

FINOCCHIO | FENNEL

We mainly use finocchio, or fennel, at La Cacciata for the abundant leaves of the wild plant; this could almost be said to be the dominant flavour of the local cooking. Unless you grow it, the leafy fennel is hard to find, so if we wish to cook Pollo Orvietano (see page 140), for example, then there will be a lot of bulb fennel left over. Incidentally, the leaf or feather fennel used in Italy does not have an edible bulb, but its dried flowers are used to flavour grilled fish.

Finocchio alla Griglia
Grilled Fennel

Or it can be translated in slang as 'grilled homosexual'!

4 people
4 small or 2 large fennel bulbs
very good olive oil
salt and pepper

Heat the ridged grill pan or barbecue to medium. Trim the outer layers of leaves and tops carefully off the fennel bulbs (do not discard these, but wrap and freeze, they can be used to good effect in fish broths and soups). Shave the base of the fennel with a potato peeler to clean it; you want the base to hold the leaves together, so do not cut. Divide the fennel bulbs into quarters longitudinally, using a sharp knife, but be careful or the quarters will break up into separate layers.

Grill the fennel quarters for approximately 5 minutes on each flat face and 5 minutes on the rounded outer side. Do not play with them, but leave alone until it is time to turn. Serve warm or at room temperature, having adjusted the seasoning. Offer oil and lemon juice.

ZUCCHINI | COURGETTES

Always choose courgettes that are very fresh, as old ones taste bitter. They should be firm, usually dark green, and glossy. Yellowing and wrinkling indicate age. Size is not that important, except that the very big ones are virtually marrows and need different treatment.

Zucchini alla Griglia
Grilled Courgettes

For your sanity, choose medium to large courgettes, as the slicing process is tedious.

1 medium–large courgette
    per person
salt and pepper
very good olive oil
lemon wedges

Cut the courgettes lengthways into slices of 3 mm thick. Arrange them neatly on the preheated ridged grill pan. Grill until the top side starts sweating and burn marks show through. Because courgettes are all water, this takes longer than other vegetables, at least 5 minutes. Season and turn and grill the reverse side for 3–4 minutes. Transfer to a serving dish and lightly oil. Adjust the seasoning, and serve with lemon wedges.

Zucchini Ripieni
Stuffed Courgettes

This dish is best used in combination with other stuffed vegetables.

4 medium, very fresh courgettes
good olive oil
1 medium onion, peeled and minced
10 basil leaves or a small
    handful of parsley leaves
4 sun-dried tomatoes in oil
    (plus their oil)
zest of 1 lemon
100 g Crisp Breadcrumbs
    (see page 189)
1 garlic clove, peeled
salt and pepper

Preheat the oven to 180°C/350°F/Gas 4. Lightly oil and moisten a baking dish or Swiss roll tin with 2 tbsp water.

Trim the ends of the courgettes and then cut in half lengthways. With a teaspoon hollow out the courgette halves. This is best done by scraping the spoon towards you holding it near vertically along the length of the courgette – imagine you are making a Polynesian war canoe. Reserve the scrapings. Arrange the courgette halves in the prepared dish in a single layer. They should fit snugly enough to hold each other up.

Heat the frying pan to high then add a little oil and the onions, followed by the courgette scrapings. Sauté briskly for 2–3 minutes. Tip this mixture into a food processor. Add the basil, tomatoes, lemon zest, most of the breadcrumbs, the garlic and a little oil. Process briefly, taste and season.

Spoon this mixture into the dug-out courgettes, drizzle with oil and scatter a small amount of the reserved breadcrumbs over. Bake for 25 minutes, making sure the baking dish does not dry up with the courgettes starting to fry and burn; add more water if necessary. Do not let them burn on top. Check for doneness by piercing the end of the courgettes with a knife. If very tender, it is done.

Fiori Fritti
Deep-fried Courgette Flowers

Throughout the summer, Rosa, the most memorable of the market traders in Orvieto, sells me several large bunches of male courgette flowers. The market is Thursday morning, and the Thursday evening class is by and large ruined by the ritual of me deep-frying these flowers and feeding them to guests during the class. Of course they must have some wine with these, and then general levels of attentiveness and diligence decline rapidly.

The reason I serve these in the kitchen rather than attempting to make a first course of them is that I can only fry a few at a time. To attempt to fry and serve twenty portions would result in a large quantity of rather cold and soggy courgette flowers. They should be eaten as soon after frying as possible.

For every courgette grown, there are two flowers present on the plant: a male flower with no fruit, and a female flower attached to the courgette. Why we are not flooded with courgette flowers in this country escapes me. In Italy, courgettes are always sold with the flower attached, but these are almost always stuffed or chopped into risotti. The male flowers with their little spiky stalks lend themselves to being dipped in a light batter and being lowered gingerly by the stalk into hot oil. (Incidentally, other squash blossoms will do equally well.)

4 courgette flowers per person
type 00 flour
sunflower oil for deep-frying
wedges of lemon

For the batter:
1 size 2 egg
250 ml cold lager
1 pinch bicarbonate of soda
salt and pepper
115 g type 00 flour

Prepare the flowers just before cooking. At the base of the flower where it is attached to the stalk, there are some spiky little leaves; remove these. If you wish to be incredibly fussy, also remove the stamens from the middle of the flowers as these have a saffron-like substance on them that can occasionally taste bitter. In my experience, only wilted flowers taste bitter, so extreme freshness avoids this tedious chore.

To make the batter, combine the egg, lager, bicarbonate, a pinch of salt and the flour in a bowl and whisk until barely mixed. Overwhisking will result in an uninteresting and heavy batter. (This, incidentally, is the principle behind the Japanese tempura.) Sprinkle more flour on to a plate, and season to taste with salt and pepper.

The best thing to fry in is a wok or a very stable large frying pan. You will need to have all your ingredients ready, as well as a tray with absorbent paper to briefly drain the flowers before eating; a pair of tongs to turn and remove the flowers from the oil, and a spider to clean the oil of any stray bits of batter between cooking. The oil used is not olive oil, but sunflower oil, and you will need a fairly large bottle. I add just a little olive oil when hot to give flavour. Heat to 180°C/350°F. The best way of testing this is to drop a little of the batter in; if it smokes, sputters slightly and turns golden, it is at the correct temperature. If it browns quickly, the oil is a little too hot; turn the heat down and add a little more oil.

Deep-frying is a potentially hazardous occupation, particularly in a wide, shallow frying pan. You only need 2 cm of oil in the pan. Do not have young children underfoot when doing this.

When the oil reaches the correct temperature, dust 8 courgette flowers by dredging them through the plate of seasoned flour. Holding them by their stalks, dunk quickly into the batter, drain slightly, then allow to float in the hot oil. After a minute or so, using the tongs, separate the flowers and attempt to turn them over. As the courgette flowers are often full of extremely hot air by this time, they tend to resist this, but persist. Continue cooking for another 2 minutes, then remove from the oil and place on the absorbent paper to drain slightly. Your guests will be descending like a pack of hyenas on this tray. Make them squeeze their own lemon over, and get on with the next batch, as this first one will disappear in seconds.

Between batches, remove any small particles of detached batter. These are delicious in their own right. A medium heat under the frying pan is the safest. It may take a minute or two for the oil to return to the correct temperature between batches, but this is preferable to burning the oil.

Little **Tip**

■ Be very careful where you put the frying pan with the hot oil after you have finished all the flowers. I place it deep underneath the cooker at La Cacciata so that there is no possibility of it being knocked over and burning anyone. An hour later, when it is cool, I make a judgement as to whether the oil is re-usable or not. Dark burnt colour or black particles indicate not; a clear oil can be used for making chips or sautéing potatoes, or browning meat.

CIPOLLE | ONIONS

My preferred onions for these recipes are the Italian white onions, smaller than our Spanish onions. Incidentally they are the same species, strength and taste as the red ones more widely available, but I find that the red ones don't look very appetising when cooked.

Cipolle alla Griglia
Grilled Onion Slices

Everyone likes the aroma of grilling onions.

2 large Spanish type onions, peeled
very good olive oil
salt and pepper

Heat a ridged grill pan or barbecue to medium, and have ready 10–12 bamboo skewers soaked in water (get these in a Chinese supermarket).

Slice the onions horizontally 1 cm thick; you should have 8–12 slices. Carefully insert the skewers through the side of each onion slice. This will hold all the rings together on the grill as they cook. Lightly brush with oil and season. Grill on one side for 10 minutes, but do not touch at all. The onion 'steaks' must be brown and showing signs of shrinking and weeping on the upper raw surfaces. When you are sure this stage has been reached, turn the onion steaks and give them 10 minutes more on the other side. Remove to a serving dish. Withdraw the skewers and dress the onions with a little oil.

Cipolle Ripiene
Stuffed Onions

This is an adaptation of a recipe by Anna del Conte. The recipe involves quite a bit of work, and may seem daunting, but if you boil the onions in advance, even the day before, to actually prep them only takes about 15 minutes. You can then either cook them in advance and serve at room temperature (surprisingly good), or hold and cook when you need them, providing it is on the same day. Believe me, this dish is worth it. The guests at La Cacciata watch me demonstrating and look very dubious, but when they get a chance to try making it themselves, they are half hooked, and eating them with a selection of other stuffed vegetables at lunch completes the addiction.

4 people
4 medium white onions, unpeeled
100 g fresh white breadcrumbs
150 ml milk

Put a pan of water on to boil with the onions in it. When the water comes to the boil, turn down the heat and simmer for 25 minutes. Turn off the heat, and leave the onions to cool in the water.

good olive oil
a handful of fresh parsley, chopped
150 g canned tuna, drained and flaked
1/4 red chilli pepper
1/2 tbsp capers, rinsed and drained
9 canned anchovy fillets, drained
1 garlic clove, peeled and minced
2 tsp dried oregano
salt and pepper if needed

Make the breadcrumbs, and mix most of them with the milk, reserving 4 tsp for the top of the stuffed onions.

Preheat the oven to 180°C/350°F/Gas 4.

When the onions are cool, peel off the outer layer of skin. Trim the root end very carefully, just enough to make it presentable, and to form a small flat base. Trim the top of the onion and discard. Now the fun bit: cut the top quarters off the onions and set aside, then carefully make four onion bowls by removing the centres. The bowl walls need to be two layers thick. Arrange the onion cups in a lightly oiled roasting dish with a few tbsp of water in the base.

Chop the onion centres and caps finely. In a frying pan heat a tbsp or so of olive oil and sauté the onion pieces until golden brown over a very high heat. Put in a food processor along with the milk-soaked breadcrumbs, the parsley, tuna, chilli, capers, anchovies, garlic and oregano. Process until a coarse paste, then taste and adjust seasoning, but as it contains anchovies and chilli, it should need neither salt nor pepper.

Spoon this mixture into the onions, heaping it up. Sprinkle the tops with the reserved dry crumbs and moisten with a little oil. Bake for 30 minutes in the preheated oven, being careful that the roasting dish doesn't dry out; if it does, add 2 tbsp water. Be careful too that the top of the stuffing doesn't burn; if this seems to be happening, cover loosely with a bit of oiled foil.

Little **Tip**

- Incidentally, the onions are very floppy and difficult to remove from the roasting dish, so, if possible, cook and serve in the same one. (Saves washing up as well.)

FUNGHI | MUSHROOMS

In an ideal world, the mushrooms here would be fresh porcini or ceps, preferably large, preferably picked by yourself. This is obviously not always possible. Dried will not do, so substitute mature cultivated common mushrooms, known in the trade as flats. (Impress your greengrocer with this arcane terminology.)

Funghi alla Griglia
Grilled Mushrooms

This recipe works particularly well with over-mature mushrooms that have flattened out and have rather black gills. Their flavour is superb.

12 large flat mushrooms
    (or ceps or porcini if you can
    afford or pick)
2 tbsp Gremolata (see page 125)
top-quality olive oil
salt and pepper

Heat a barbecue or ridged grill pan.

Remove the stalks from the mushrooms, and in the case of the flats, peel the caps; simply wipe ceps with a damp cloth. Stems from flats are useful in stocks; stems from ceps should be cut lengthways and grilled along with the caps.

Grill the caps top side down until water collects in the hole where the stalk was. This will take 8–10 minutes. Turn the mushrooms and grill for 2 minutes on the other side. Transfer to a serving dish, and scatter with gremolata, salt, pepper and olive oil. They will give out copious and delicious juices, so sop them up with bread.

Funghi Ripieni
Stuffed Mushrooms

In contrast to the previous recipe, try and find large mushrooms which still form a natural bowl for the stuffing when you remove the stalks.

8 large flat mushrooms, peeled
    and stalked (keep the stalks)
good olive oil
1 small white onion or shallot,
    peeled and finely diced
2 garlic cloves, peeled and
    finely chopped
a handful of fresh parsley, chopped
200 g Crisp Breadcrumbs
    (see page 189)
salt and pepper

Preheat the oven to 180°C/350°F/Gas 4.

Chop the mushroom stalks finely. Heat a little oil in a frying pan over a medium heat, add the onion, and sweat until tender. Add the garlic, parsley and breadcrumbs, then allow to cool. Mix in a little oil and salt and pepper; the mixture should just about hold together when compressed.

Spoon this mixture into the 'bowl' of the mushrooms and arrange them in a baking dish, stuffing uppermost, in a single layer. Drizzle very lightly with oil and scatter a few drops of water on the baking tray. Bake in the preheated oven for 20 minutes or until the mushrooms have nearly collapsed and the stuffing is brown and crisp. Remove to a serving dish and pour any juices in the tray around the mushrooms.

FAGIOLI BORLOTTI | BORLOTTI BEANS

Fresh borlotti beans are available in Britain in July and August. The pods are very pretty, as are the beans inside. Unfortunately they don't maintain the bird-egg type markings when cooked.

Insalata di Borlotti Freschi
Salad of Fresh Borlotti Beans

This dish can also be made with any reconstituted dried bean; it's particularly good with dried broad beans. The amount of beans here will do two bean dishes; for a purée of the remainder, see Bruschetta, page 104.

2 kg fresh borlotti beans in the pod
2 garlic cloves, peeled
1 bay leaf
1 fresh red chilli pepper
1 celery stalk, strings removed
1 carrot, peeled
1 red onion, peeled
4 tbsp Gremolata (see page 125)
1 lemon
6 tbsp top-quality olive oil
salt and pepper

Pod the beans, cover them with water, bring to the boil and skim. Turn the heat down to a simmer, then add the garlic, bay and chilli, and simmer until the beans are fully cooked, about 40 minutes. When they are cooked, set aside in their liquor.

Prepare the vegetables, cutting them into very fine dice. Make the gremolata, using the zest of the lemon, then juice the lemon.

For the dressing, in a serving bowl heap the celery, carrot and onion dice, the lemon juice and olive oil. Season a little. Using a slotted spoon carefully drain half the beans. Add to the bowl while still hot. Toss and taste, adjust the seasoning, then add the gremolata. Serve the same day, do not refrigerate. Store the remainder of the beans in their liquor in the fridge when cold.

Little **Tip**

- Other cooked dried pulses – for example, fagioli cannellini, or ceci (chickpeas) – can be adapted to this recipe. Merely dress when warm with the vegetables, oil and gremolata.

MELANZANE | AUBERGINES/EGGPLANTS

Only buy spanking fresh, firm, blooming and thoroughly sexy aubergines. Prod and poke, check the leafy and, incidentally, spiky stem. If the leaves are withered and old, so is the aubergine; if they are crisp, and hard to prise away from the fruit, good. An old aubergine is a bitter and twisted aubergine, and no amount of salting will alleviate this psychological condition. Salting a fresh aubergine is another matter; that removes liquid and in many dishes improves the texture.

Look out for the pale Italian aubergines in the summer, they are the works. Avoid very small aubergines that are used in other cuisines, the Italians on the whole prefer the big ones. Aubergine skin will blunt any knife (as will tomato skin), so use a serrated knife for slicing and cutting.

Melanzane alla Griglia
Grilled Aubergines

This is best made with the large, pale mauve, summer aubergines.

2 aubergines
salt and pepper
very good olive oil
Gremolata (see page 125)

Slice the aubergines either horizontally 1 cm thick or into rounds of the same thickness. Heat the ridged grill pan to medium, or allow the barbecue to die down a bit. Lightly salt the aubergines and individually brush with oil, not lightly, but not extravagantly.

Grill the slices of aubergine for 3–4 minutes on each side; you will need to do this in at least two batches. When done, remove to a large plate and spread out, scatter with gremolata, drizzle with a little more oil and adjust seasoning to taste.

Melanzane Ripiene
Stuffed Aubergines

This is a reworking of a reworking by Richard Whittington of Imam Bayildi.

4 aubergines, medium–large
good olive oil
salt and pepper
6 tbsp Tomato Sauce (see page 189)
1 onion, peeled and coarsely
    chopped into about 5 mm dice
1 garlic clove, peeled and minced
a handful of parsley leaves, chopped
50 g Crisp Breadcrumbs
    (see page 189)

- The amount of oil used in this dish should be very judicious. Aubergines absorb oil like sponges in the early stages of cooking and exude it as a greasy mess later – remember moussaka.

Preheat the oven to its maximum, and lightly oil a baking sheet.

Cut the aubergines in half longitudinally, season and arrange on the baking sheet, cut or flat surface down. Bake for 20 minutes in the preheated oven, then remove and allow to cool. Prepare the tomato sauce. Sauté the onion very briefly and fiercely in a little oil, then add the garlic and parsley. Mix into the tomato sauce. When the aubergines are cool enough to handle, very carefully scoop out about half the flesh, coarsely chop it, then mix with the tomato sauce mixture. Taste this and season, and you might possibly add a little oil.

Very carefully arrange the emptied-out aubergine skins or shells in a lightly oiled roasting or gratin dish. All the way through this book I will bang on about selecting the correct sized dish for a particular recipe. Nowhere is this more essential than here. The eight floppy, incredibly fragile aubergine skins must fit snugly into the selected dish. Spoon the stuffing into the skins, scatter with the breadcrumbs and drizzle lightly with some oil. Return to the oven and bake until hot, brown, crisp and bubbling, about 15 minutes. Serve in the roasting dish.

POMODORI | TOMATOES

Nothing shouts Italian cooking more than tomatoes. What did they cook with before Columbus discovered the New World and brought back tomatoes, peppers and chillies, all three now absolutely irreplaceable on the average trattoria menu.

In Italian cooking most recipes can use tinned tomatoes. Where fresh are called for, as here, some care and shopping are necessary. Watery, mass-produced tomatoes will not do. Supermarkets now sell plum and vine-ripened tomatoes nearly all year round, but they still lack flavour and ripeness. The solution is to buy a good quality tomato four to five days in advance of doing the recipe. Spread out on an attractive plate and keep out of the fridge in your kitchen. A sunny windowsill would be ideal. You may lose the odd one, but this is a small price to pay for proper tomatoes.

The bar in my restaurant in Frith Street provides an almost perfect ambiance for ripening tomatoes. Perhaps cigarette fumes contribute to the ripening process . . .

Pomodori Ripieni con Pesto Pangrattato

Tomatoes with Pesto Breadcrumbs

Serve as part of an antipasti, and these tomatoes are also excellent as a garnish for roast lamb.

10 ripe plum tomatoes
very good olive oil
salt and pepper
a large handful of basil
    (have plenty to hand)
50 g Parmesan, grated
50 g pine nuts
100 g Crisp Breadcrumbs
    (see page 189)
2 garlic cloves, peeled

Preheat the oven to 140–150°C/275–300°F/Gas 1–2. Oil a baking tray or gratin dish just big enough to hold the tomatoes in a single layer. Moisten this tray with a little water.

Cut the tomatoes in half longitudinally, and scoop out the seeds (one use for a melon baller, but a teaspoon is better). Season lightly and leave like inverted boats, on a rack over a plate, to drain.

To make the pesto crumbs, combine the basil, Parmesan, pine nuts, breadcrumbs and garlic in a food processor. Whizz, then add enough oil so that the mix will lightly cohere when pressed. Check the seasoning.

Stuff the tomatoes with this mix (do not heap it up), and arrange carefully in the prepared gratin dish. Sprinkle with a little coarse salt, a few extra breadcrumbs and a little oil. Bake in the preheated oven for 40 minutes until the tomatoes are collapsed. Do not allow them to burn on top (you may cover loosely with foil once brown, but this will cause the crust to steam and not remain crisp). Do not allow the water in the dish to completely dry out, or the tomatoes will burn on the bottom.

The cooking times are approximate. You must learn to make your own judgements; remember that tomatoes are good raw and delicious cooked, but an indeterminate halfway stage is not pleasant.

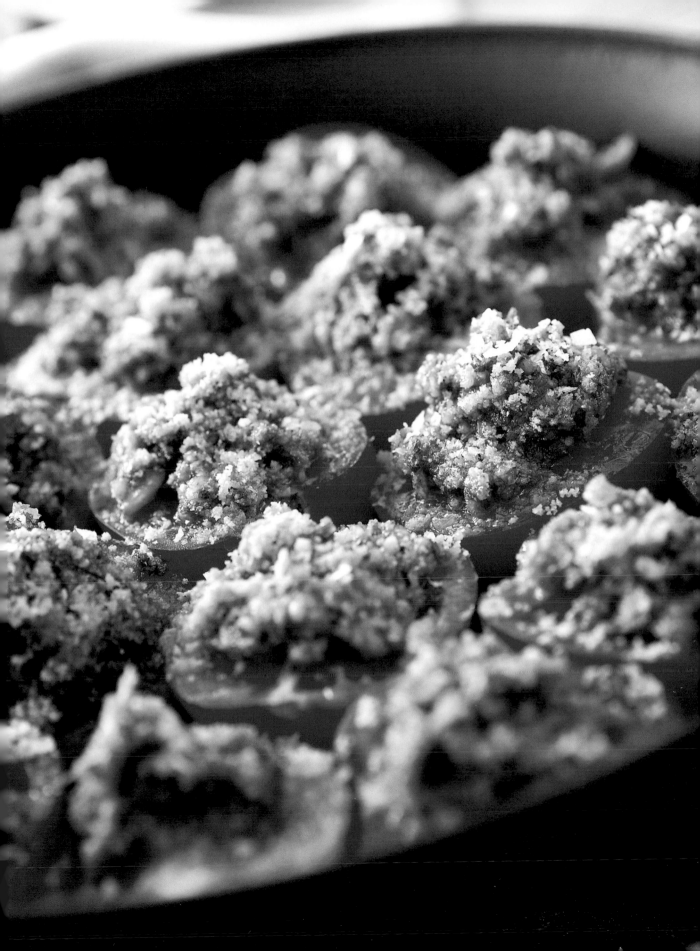

Pomodori alla Griglia
Grilled Tomatoes

10 plum tomatoes, halved
    lengthways
very good olive oil
salt and pepper

Build a very hot barbecue, or superheat a ridged grill pan. Brush the tomatoes lightly with oil, and season on the flat cut surface. Carefully put the tomato halves, cut side down, on the grill, then do not attempt to move them for at least 8 minutes. They will char and shrink, but should not be stuck (too much). After 8–10 minutes, gingerly turn them over and give them another 5 minutes. Remove to a serving dish, season if necessary, and sprinkle with oil. They taste better at room temperature.

Pomodori Secchi
Oven-dried Tomatoes

Dissatisfaction with the quality of sun-dried tomatoes available led to experimentation with home-drying. The results are splendid. Such a simple, easy but slightly lengthy process has an almost alchemical effect on the tomatoes.

20 ripe plum tomatoes
salt and pepper
sugar

Little Variant

- Have ready 12 Oven-dried Tomatoes, and preheat the oven to 150°C/300°F/Gas 2.
    Mix 100 g Crisp Breadcrumbs (see page 189) with a handful of chopped fresh basil and a little oil from the tomatoes, and season with salt and pepper. Top the tomatoes with this mixture, and place in a suitable dish. Drizzle lightly with some of the oil from the tomatoes, and bake in the preheated oven for 20 minutes.

Preheat the oven to 150°C/300°F/Gas 2. Lightly moisten a baking sheet.

Halve the tomatoes and scoop out the seeds. Arrange the tomato halves, flat side up, in a single layer on the baking sheet. Sprinkle carefully with coarse salt, coarse pepper and a very small amount of sugar. Bake dry in the preheated oven for 1 1/2–2 hours. They will cook at an uneven rate so from time to time reposition them, bringing the rawer ones to the outside of the tray. (Baking trays tend to warp and form a swamp in the bottom; a large Le Creuset gratin dish is therefore the best for this type of cooking, as only a French nuclear test would warp it.) Allow to cool. Store if not needed in a jar covered in very good olive oil in the fridge.

FAGIOLINI | GREEN BEANS

Any fresh and tender green beans can be used for this recipe. At La Cacciata we buy at various points throughout the season runner beans, bobby beans, and then finally French beans. The cooking time will vary slightly, according to type.

Fagiolini con Aceto Balsamico e Olio di Tartufo
Green Beans with Balsamic Vinegar and Truffle Oil

A cold antipasto, which is stunning in its simplicity. This dressing method also works really well for delicate salads such as rocket. Dress and serve immediately.

500 g French beans or runner
    beans, topped and tailed
salt and pepper
balsamic vinegar
truffle oil

Bring 1 litre water to the boil and salt heavily. Prepare the beans and put in a blanching basket. Place into the boiling water, and boil until tender, then remove immediately and dip into cold water. When cool, drain thoroughly and reserve until needed. It is very important they are well drained otherwise they dislike the dressing.

Take a serving bowl and put 4–5 drops balsamic vinegar in the bottom. Add nearly three times this much of the truffle oil. Season liberally. Put the beans in the bowl and toss swiftly. Taste for seasoning, adjust if necessary, and serve. The beans will discolour if dressed in advance, and the flavour of the oil will dissipate.

INSALATE
SALADS

The following salads are salads in the chef sense rather than in the mixed leaf sense. They make perfectly good lunch dishes or starters. Most Italians will cheerfully sit down to two three-course meals a day, but I've had the greatest difficulty in persuading the guests at La Cacciata that this is a good thing for their figures. Frequently lunch will be a light pasta, and one of these dishes, with fruit or cheese to follow.

The idea of a mixed salad seems alien to Italian cooking. If you order a salad in a restaurant, you will normally be served cos lettuce with olive oil and lemon. Jolly nice too. Because of the seasonality of the Italian vegetable markets, you rarely see a vast range of mixed designer leaves. Only one of the leaves will be in season, and sold at a time, and that is what will be served.

The small peasant stalls in Orvieto market do, however, sell selections of rather bitter wild and cultivated leaves under the general heading of cicoria. These are a bit of an acquired taste, but I find them delicious.

Insalata di Verdure alla Griglia
Grilled Vegetable Salad

This is a sophisticated dish, using a number of the previous recipes in the Antipasti di Verdura section – dinner party stuff.

4–6 people

Prepare half recipes for:
grilled courgettes
grilled aubergines
grilled peppers (see below)
grilled onions

Additionally:
24 stoned black olives
24 Oven-dried Tomatoes (see
    page 32) or good quality sun-
    dried tomatoes with their oil
2 buffalo mozzarella

Mix all together, except for the mozzarella, and check the seasoning. Serve mounded in soup plates, but remember this is a starter, so not too big a portion. Grate the mozzarella over the vegetable salad. Serve with bruschetta if you insist.

■ **Leftovers make a wonderful pizza topping.**

Insalata di Peperoni alla Griglia
Grilled Pepper Salad

Under no circumstances use green peppers for this dish. They are merely unripe red peppers, and will give you chronic wind.

4 people
2 medium red and 2 medium
    yellow peppers
salt and pepper
a handful of fresh basil
top-quality olive oil

Cook the peppers directly over the flame. Turn them occasionally until the skin is completely black and blistered. Do not be faint-hearted; cook them on the highest heat, char them until you think they are overdone, and then blacken them some more. Remove to a bowl, clingfilm the top, and leave the peppers to steam and cool for 30 minutes.

Peel quickly under running water, using the colander to catch the copious charred skin, and prevent it blocking your sink. Do not immerse the peppers in water, merely use the running water to help the cleaning process.

Shake the peppers dry. Cut in half lengthways and remove and discard the stem, seeds and pith. Trim the flesh into rectangles of 2 x 6 cm, and place in a serving dish. When all have been done, season and add the basil, and dress with unbelievably good oil.

Insalata di Verdure Arroste

Insalata di Verdure Arroste
Salad of Roasted Vegetables

The sight of the first Italian lemons, complete with their leaves, prompts me to make this dish, illustrated on the previous page, every year. Of all the roast, baked, grilled or marinated vegetable dishes in this book, this is my favourite. An atypical selection of vegetables is used – no tomato, aubergine, courgette, bell peppers or basil. Those used are of North European cooking – potatoes, turnips, peas etc. – but they are seasoned with the flavours of the Mediterranean – olive oil, chillies, lemon juice and garlic. In short a mongrel of a dish. It can be served as an antipasto or as a contorno (accompaniment). This is the dish in which to use all those infantile vegetables the supermarkets so proudly stock.

6–8 people
300 g new potatoes, scrubbed and
    cut into bite-sized pieces
200 g baby or small bunch carrots,
    peeled and split lengthways if
    larger than bite-sized
1 kg peas, podded
200 g baby summer turnips,
    washed and quartered
300 g asparagus stalks, peeled and
    trimmed
2 bunches large spring onions,
    partially split from the green end
    and rinsed thoroughly
200 g button mushrooms,
    preferably chestnut brown,
    quartered
6 cooked baby artichokes (optional,
    see page 14), quartered
very good olive oil
5 lemons, with leaves if possible
4 garlic cloves, peeled and grated
1 large red chilli pepper, seeded and
    very finely diced
sea salt and pepper
2 bay leaves

The list of vegetables is not definitive. Buy what is in season, but avoid beetroot as it colours everything else. Spinach, runner beans, pickling onions, greens, French beans and many others can be included. No baby sweetcorn please, I loathe it.

We are going to blanch and refresh a large selection of vegetables, so a little assembling of equipment and organisation is appropriate. Put 4 litres of water on to boil. Take two large bowls and half fill one with cold water. Put a colander in the empty bowl. Find your spider or buy one; it's an absolutely essential piece of kit.

Blanch the potatoes, carrots, peas and turnip in the unsalted water for 10–12 minutes. They should be al dente, i.e. cooked, but with a little residual resistance to the bite. Drain with the spider and refresh in cold water. Drain again with the spider and transfer to the colander.

In the 10 minutes or so that the first batch of vegetables are cooking, prepare the asparagus (and broad beans, French beans or runner beans if using). While you are draining the first batch, the water must be left on a high heat to return to a boil. Blanch the asparagus (and beans) for 4–5 minutes, drain with the spider, refresh, drain again and add to the other vegetables in the colander. (You may need to change the water in the refreshing bowl and to tip out the excess water collecting below the colander in the other bowl.)

Prepare the spring onions and mushrooms and blanch for 1 minute, then refresh and add to the vegetables in the colander. (If you are cooking spinach, this should be in this batch.) Let the vegetables sit to drain then mix thoroughly and return to the dried-out bowl. They will look brilliant – but don't worry, we are going to fix that.

At this point the vegetables can be held for up to one day, well drained and clingfilmed in the fridge. If you do this, give them 10 minutes in a colander when it is time to finish the dish as they will have rendered more water during their sojourn in the fridge.

When ready to roast, preheat the oven to its maximum. Select a large roasting dish and lightly oil it.

Quarter the artichokes and add to the other vegetables. Into a bowl (the refreshing bowl washed and dried), squeeze 2 of the lemons, then add the minced garlic and chilli and 100 ml olive oil. Mix thoroughly then tip in all the vegetables. Season with coarse black pepper and sea salt and mix everything thoroughly. You may need a little more oil. Add the bay leaves. If you have lemon leaves, add them at this point.

Lightly drizzle the vegetables in the prepared roasting dish with oil, transfer to the oven, and roast for 30 minutes. Do not stir, as you want the protruding vegetables to brown and dry in the hot oven. You may shake the roasting dish from time to time to prevent sticking. Remove from the oven and allow to cool at least partially, as to my mind this dish is best at room temperature.

To serve, select a large, pretty, serving platter and tip the vegetables on to it. They will have lost their vibrant colours but the improved flavours imbued by roasting in a dressing will more than compensate. Serve with half lemons and more olive oil to taste.

Little **Variant**

- Make a dressing with the olive oil and lemon juice, omitting the chilli and garlic. Roast the vegetables dressed with this. When done add 4 tbsp of the Cep and Truffle Relish on page 77, toss thoroughly, allow to cool a little, and serve warm.

Insalata di Rucola e Tartufo
Salad of Rocket and Truffle

Difficult one, this one – expensive too. What sort of truffle? In Umbria during summer there is a relatively abundant truffle known to its friends as *Tuber aestivum* or summer truffle. It is also comparatively inexpensive over there, about £100 a kilo or £2–3 a portion. It freezes well and is normally served raw, grated directly on to food straight from the freezer. Buy some if you get a chance in Italy, wrap them in tissue, put in a jar and refrigerate. Freeze individually, clingfilm wrapped, when you get them home. Use by Christmas.

That's the truffle sorted out, now the rocket. The correct leaf for this dish is *Eruca sativa*, wild rocket. In fact this means any small, very strong rocket. I hope by the time this book comes out that supermarkets will sell rocket in realistic quantities and treat it like a salad and not like a herb.

4–6 people

4 large handfuls small strong rocket
    (as opposed to large floppy-
    leafed, weak and feeble rocket)
60 g summer truffle
1/2 tsp balsamic vinegar
3 tsp truffle oil
salt and pepper
fresh Parmesan, flaked (shaved
    freshly with a potato peeler)

Take a medium salad bowl and pour the balsamic vinegar in. Add the truffle oil, plus salt and pepper fairly generously. Take your truffle and through the medium holes of a grater (usually on the side), grate the truffle into the bowl. Remove any truffle that clings to the inside of the grater carefully with a small knife, and add to the bowl. Put in the rocket and very gently toss and stir the rocket until it has 'cleaned' the bowl. You are in essence dressing the salad bowl and then lightly wiping it with the salad leaves. This is a very effective technique for not flattening and subduing delicate salads.

Arrange the unbelievably aromatic rocket on four small plates and shave a few slivers of Parmesan over.

This salad is a good starter in its own right. It is delicious on lightly oiled Bruschetta (see page 104) and is even more extraordinary on the Potato Pizza (see page 102). Just make the pizza and plop some salad on to it.

Insalata di Prezzemolo e Verdure Grigliate
Grilled Vegetable and Parsley Salad

The Italians regard parsley as an aphrodisiac so the Two Gentlemen of Orvieto I first served this dish to, got rather excited about it (not that Italian males seem to need any help in that direction). You will need to prepare a small quantity of grilled vegetables from the various recipes already given and in addition some crostini (stale are fine). Sorry about all the cross references.

This salad is a good use of leftover grilled vegetables, but is much better with freshly grilled, still warm ones. There is a certain magic about cooked vegetables dressed whilst still warm that a cold assemblage lacks. If you doubt this, try dressing potato salad whilst the potatoes are still steaming.

6–8 people
2 grilled courgettes (see page 21)
2 grilled red peppers (see page 34)
1 grilled yellow pepper (see page 34)
1 grilled aubergine (see page 29)
1 large bunch continental parsley,
    leaves picked, washed and dried
    in a salad spinner
1 tbsp red wine vinegar
4 tbsp good olive oil, including the oil
    from the tomatoes
12 sun-dried tomatoes in oil
1 handful stoned black olives
1 tbsp desalinated and rinsed capers
salt and pepper
Crisp Breadcrumbs (see page 189)

To make the dressing combine the vinegar and oil in a large salad bowl. Coarsely chop the tomatoes and olives and add, followed finally by the capers. Season with black pepper and a little salt.

To assemble the salad, put the vegetables and parsley in the bowl with the dressing and toss. Pile into mounds on four plates and scatter 2 tbsp of the crispy crumbs on top of each one. The crumbs provide extra texture and absorb excess oil.

CARPACCIO

Carpaccio, the man, was a Venetian painter (1472–1526) given to rather religious scenes and showing a fondness in his painting for young men with improbably long legs and taut, hose-clad buttocks. Carpaccio, the dish, is a much copied raw beef dish from Harry's Bar, an equally precious Venetian institution. Whimsy is a speciality at Arrigo Cipriani's bar: whimsy in the size of the bills presented to his essentially non-Italian clientele, and whimsy in naming his dishes and drinks after Venetian painters (viz, Bellini).

Carpaccio, the dish, was originally very, very rare roast sirloin sliced thinly after trimming off the cooked edge and dressed with a rather unpleasant mayonnaise-based sauce. The price was approximately the gross domestic product of a small third-world dictatorship and was only eaten by rich (and stupid) foreigners like me. However, some of these foreigners were cooks and took the idea with them. The sump-oil sauce disappeared, and rocket, truffles, Parmesan, good oil, lemon and various other ingredients were added – although not usually at the same time (unless Tony Worrall Thompson was serving it). It was not restricted to beef. I have even seen a carpaccio of lobster on a menu. Franco Taruschio at the Walnut Tree does it with veal and white truffle. Wolfgang Puck did it with anything. I stick to beef or cured pork, and even have a vegetarian Carpaccio of Zucchini. About ten years ago the version involving a bed of rocket returned to Italy and is now all conquering.

Carpaccio di Manzo
Carpaccio of Beef Fillet

I recommend this dish as a summer main course. The meat is beef fillet which is heavily seasoned, grilled over a very high heat for 1 minute on each face then plunged into iced water to arrest the cooking. The cooked outer crust so fatuously discarded at Harry's Bar is retained as it is the 'best bit'.

6 people
400–500 g fillet of beef
    chateaubriand, in one piece,
    ask your butcher to trim
    off any fat or sinew
salt and pepper
Salad of Rocket and Truffle (see
    page 38)
Parmesan, in the piece
very good olive oil

Heat a ridged grill pan to nearly melting. Prepare a bowl of iced water. Season the meat with salt and pepper very generously. Grill the beef on each face for 1 minute. Remove and douse in iced water. As soon as it is cool remove, pat dry and refrigerate. Don't worry about the heavy-handed seasoning, most of it comes off on the grill or rinses off in the water. You now have a choice: thickish or thin.

'Thick' Carpaccio di Manzo

Make the rocket salad and arrange on your best large serving dish. With a U-shaped potato peeler make about two dozen Parmesan shavings. Slice the meat vertically across the cylindrically shaped piece of meat. You should try and do this as thinly as you can using a thin, long knife, preferably very sharp.

Arrange these slices of meat on the bed of rocket; there should be about four per person. Drizzle with top-quality olive oil, season lightly and scatter with Parmesan slivers. Serve immediately (do not refrigerate).

'Thin', Slightly Cured Carpaccio di Manzo

You will need some sheets of greaseproof paper and a meat bat (a cleaver, mallet or even a child's wooden hammer – you know, the one they bang their thumbs with when missing the pegs in holes).

Slice the meat as for 'thick' carpaccio. Lightly oil a sheet of greaseproof paper and season lightly. Arrange four slices of beef on this, at least 5 cm apart. Oil and season another sheet of paper and put the prepared side down on top of the meat. Gently bat the slices of meat until they have spread out to at least twice their former size. Repeat this procedure until all the meat is prepared. Refrigerate until needed. The seasoning will partially cure the meat and it holds for two to three days in the fridge.

Serve in the same way as 'thick' carpaccio or like bresaola, covering a plate with coarsely ground black pepper or a few drops of the Cep and Truffle Relish on page 77, or finely grated summer truffle.

Carpaccio di Coppa (Bresaola)
Carpaccio of Coppa Salami (Marinated Beef)

You will need 4 good slices of coppa salami per person with no trace of skin or crust around their rim (or bresaola). Proceed in exactly the same way as for 'thick' Carpaccio di Manzo, except you should offer some lemon wedges.

Carpaccio di Zucchini
Carpaccio of Courgettes

I've never been particularly fond of vegetarian dishes where an attempt is made to replace meat with a substitute. (Soyaburgers spring to mind.) This is the exception. It is best made at the last minute.

4 people
4 medium courgettes, very
    fresh and about 10 cm long
Salad of Rocket and Truffle (see
    page 38)
1 lemon
salt and pepper
Parmesan, in the piece
very good olive oil

Top and tail the courgettes. Slice them longitudinally as thinly as you can (preferably with a mandolin, but be careful with your fingers). Discard the first and last slices as they have too much skin on.

Make the rocket salad. Arrange the courgettes on a tray and squeeze the lemon juice all over them. Season, and then arrange on the rocket. Throw away any lemon juice remaining on the tray. Shave the Parmesan cheese on top, and drizzle with a little oil.

SALAME, BRESAOLA E PROSCIUTTO
CURED MEAT ANTIPASTI

The best meat antipasto I've ever eaten was the result of a casual request to Lucio Sforza in his Orvieto restaurant to provide some nibbles for my guests while they waited for a couple of shopping stragglers. The slicer went into overdrive: home-made wind-dried horsemeat, turkey leg ham, donkey salami, local wild boar loin, smoked lard, speck, prosciutto, pancetta and cured lamb all appeared with bewildering rapidity. I was sure their British sensibilities would be overwhelmed and nauseated, not so; country housewives chomped their horsemeat in blissful ignorance. There is, of course, no need to go to this extreme when providing a salami course, just offer freshly sliced ham and salami with some good olives. Please avoid those packets of pre-sliced meats so beloved of our wonderful supermarkets; the later a salami is sliced the rosier the colour and the better it will taste. When they turn dull, browny red, they have oxidised and are past it.

Offer a balanced selection of four types. One prosciutto or coppa (shoulder, from the same animals as prosciutto), one softer sausage, say Felino; one harder sausage such as Milano or Napoli; and one other, possibly bresaola. Get your delicatessen to slice them as late as feasible and keep in an airtight zip-lock bag until serving. Lay the meats out on a large platter, and season with some freshly grated black pepper and a few dribbles of your best olive oil.

Lardo Stagionato
Seasoned Lard

'Lardo stagionato' literally means seasoned and aged lard. It's salt-back fat from flavoursome pigs, sliced wafer thin then seasoned with rosemary, olive oil and black pepper. It's served prettily as a sashimi rose with grilled home-made bread.

6 people
225 g Italian lard (ask your
    delicatessen to slice on number
    1 and clingwrap)
top-quality olive oil
sea salt
coarsely ground black pepper
1 big sprig rosemary
home-made bread or ciabatta (see
    page 97)

Take a tray big enough to hold the lard slices flat in one layer. Cover the bottom with a little olive oil. Season lightly with sea salt and generously with pepper and rosemary leaves, then lay the fat on top. Repeat the oil and seasoning process, then leave for up to 1 day in the fridge. Arrange the fat curled on a plate like rose petals. Grill slices of bread. Serve the olive nectar separately.

Lard and a selection of salami

ANTIPASTI DI MARE
SEAFOOD ANTIPASTI

Order this dish in an Italian restaurant away from the sea, and you will undoubtedly get a jar of ghastly decomposing seafood kept in rancid soya oil. On the other hand order it in Venice or in any of the good seafood restaurants dotted around Italy's long coastline, and you will get something quite wonderful, a feast of plainly cooked fresh shellfish and molluscs, all served separately, with possibly a little mayonnaise. I suggest if you want to prepare something like this then don't serve it as a starter but make it the central feature of a summer lunch.

GAMBERI | PRAWNS
The cooked and frozen at sea North Atlantic prawns with their heads and shells on are amongst the tastiest in the world, with a far better flavour than tiger prawns or anything from hotter parts of the world. The only thing against them is their small size and fiddliness. Buy frozen and leave to defrost at room temperature for an hour before serving. Mayonnaise and lemon wedges are compulsory.

CALAMARI | SQUID
Ask your fishmonger to clean 1 kg of squid and then cut into bite-sized pieces.

Calamari 1
Put the squid pieces into a bowl with salt and a little Infused Oil (see page 187) and chopped parsley. Massage a little (disgusting) and marinate for 30 minutes.

Heat a large frying pan over a high flame. Add 3 tbsp good oil and very, very quickly fry half the squid for no more than 2 minutes, tossing once or twice. Tip out on to a serving dish, wipe out the pan with kitchen roll and repeat.

Overcooked squid goes rubbery, so the vital element here is speed. The wet squid must splutter and protest angrily as it hits the oil, indeed you may get a brief flare up. As soon as the squid begins to exude liquid it is almost too cooked. Tip out on to a serving dish and spread out to cool more quickly.

Calamari 2
Bring a large pot of water to the boil and salt it heavily. Drop the squid pieces into the water for 2 minutes maximum, then remove with a spider to a serving dish. Dress while still warm with lemon juice, olive oil, finely chopped chilli and garlic, then lashings of parsley.

POLPO | OCTOPUS
Only the tentacles can be eaten unless you are fortunate enough to find baby octopi. Ask your fishmonger to order the fish for you and prepare it. Simmer the tentacles whole in salted water for 45 minutes or until as nearly tender as they ever get. Drain and allow to cool a little, then slice into bite-sized pieces and dress as for the squid. Well worth the effort. Serve at room temperature.

VONGOLE VERACI | PALOURDE CLAMS
Simply fry them in a little sunflower oil in a large frying pan, removing them individually as they open to a serving plate. Sprinkle with coarsely chopped parsley, and serve at room temperature.

43

COZZE | MUSSELS

Hard to beat steamed open in a little dry white wine with a touch of garlic and lots of parsley. Remember not to heap mussels up in a pan, try and cook in as near a single layer as possible. The reason for this is that those on top hold the bottom ones closed and they overcook. If preparing a lot, do in batches. Serve at room temperature with their liquor.

CANNOLICCHI | RAZOR SHELLS

Should you be lucky enough to find some, cook as for the Vongole Veraci.

LUMACHE DI MARE | WHELKS

Wash and rinse under running cold water for about 30 minutes, then put in a pan with abundant cold water, a little salt and the zest of 2 lemons. Bring to the boil and leave to cook for approximately 45 minutes. Leave to cool in the liquor and drain when needed. Serve with toothpicks.

If you are able to find winkles, cook as for whelks, but for 15 minutes only.

SCAMPI, GRANCHIO E ARAGOSTA | LANGOUSTINE, CRAB AND LOBSTER

Expensive and delicious. Serve reasonably freshly boiled at room temperature with mayonnaise, lemon finger bowls, crackers, steam hammer and picks. Keep the debris, rinse it and freeze it for making fish broth. A good fishmonger will boil them for you.

BACCALA | SALT COD

Salt cod as sold in Italy and in delis here is pretty awful stuff, redolent of anatomical jokes and taking 48 hours desalinating under running water (what price metered water). It's much better doing it yourself at home.

Baccala
Home-salted Cod

This needs 2 days' preparation.

4–6 people
1.5 kg cod fillet with skin (frozen fillet
    pieces will do)
50 g Maldon salt
10 g coarsely ground black pepper
10 g caster sugar

Sprinkle the cod with salt, pepper and sugar, toss and leave in the fridge overnight. Rinse for 2 hours before using. (Taste a slice if you have doubts about the saltiness.) Use in the Salt Cod and Chickpeas (see page 150), Baccala Mantecata or the Salad of Marinated Salt Cod, Rocket and Fresh Borlotti Beans (see below).

Insalata de Baccala, Borlotti e Rucola
Salad of Marinated Salt Cod, Rocket and Fresh Borlotti Beans

At Scaletta in Milan, this dish became a notorious example of Novella Cucina, the rather lame Italian copy of Nouvelle Cuisine. Notorious because the salt cod was not cooked, merely marinated in lemon juice. However, the dish is excellent, and I have been serving it in my restaurants and at La Cacciata for years.

4–6 people

250 g desalinated Home-salted Cod
 (see opposite)
juice of 2 lemons
a large handful of good rocket
1/2 recipe borlotti bean salad (see
 page 28)
1 bunch chives, cut into 1 cm lengths
very good olive oil
coarsely ground black pepper

Have ready a glass, ceramic or stainless, wide rimmed dish. Pour the lemon juice into this. With a flexible knife, slice the salt cod fillets horizontally into as thin slices as you can manage. Pick out and discard any bones as you slice (think smoked salmon here). Lay these slices in the lemon juice for 10 minutes, turning once.

Arrange a pile of the rocket leaves in the centre of a large serving platter, then place the marinated cod around. Mound the borlotti beans on the rocket. Spoon a little of the lemon juice over the cod, then scatter the chives to contrast with the white of the fish. Drizzle with olive oil and a little pepper. Do not assemble this dish more than 5 minutes before eating.

Little **Tip**

■ If you find the idea of briefly marinated cod slightly repellent, try leaving it in the lemon juice overnight. The acidity will completely cook the cod.

Baccala Mantecata
Brandade de Morue

This dish is best made relatively close to serving. Ideally, it should be slightly warm.

4–6 people

500 g desalinated Home-salted Cod
 (see opposite)
500 ml milk
1 bay leaf
5 black peppercorns
2 garlic cloves, peeled
very good olive oil
juice of 1 lemon
black pepper
1 small bunch parsley, coarsely
 chopped

Put the cod in the milk with the bay leaf and peppercorns for about 10 minutes at a low simmer. Once it starts to bubble, take it off the heat and leave to cool in the milk.

With your fingers pick the cod out of the milk and flake it into a food processor. As you do this remove the bones and skin. Reserve the milk, then strain and add 2 tbsp of it to the cod. Add the garlic and then purée for a few seconds. Then start pouring in the olive oil in a slow stream as the machine runs. You should get about 250 ml in to form a soft purée. Add the lemon juice, ground pepper to taste and the parsley, and whirl just enough to mix. Check the seasoning and serve.

Little **Tip**

■ If the purée separates, try adding 2 more tbsp milk and whirl at maximum speed.

INSALATA DI GAMBERI
Prawn Salad

A photographic shoot at La Cacciata resulted in a large quantity of prawns being left for us to eat. This was the dish I improvised. It combines a marination, cooking, and then a secondary marination after cooking.

6 people

1 kg headless tiger prawns,

    shell on (ask your fishmonger

    for a 16–20 prawn per 500 g count)

juice of 1 lemon

salt and pepper

1 large red chilli pepper,

    seeded and finely minced

2 garlic cloves, peeled and minced

good olive oil

1 sprig parsley, chopped

2 ripe tomatoes, skinned, seeded

    and diced

1 red onion, peeled and finely diced

2 lemons

To prepare the prawns, butterfly them through the back. To do this, press each prawn flat on a chopping board, back uppermost. Carefully, with a small serrated knife, cut the shell and prawn nearly all the way through. Turn over, open the prawns out and press flat.

Arrange in a tray awaiting their marinade. Sprinkle with the lemon juice, season liberally with salt, then scatter with the chilli and garlic. Finally, add a good amount of olive oil. Marinate for up to 2 hours in the fridge.

To cook the prawns, you have two choices: ridged grill pan or a large frying pan. Place the prawns, very carefully, shell down in or on the hot pan (whatever) in a single layer fairly snugly. They are not moved after this until done and they need no extra oil, only a little of the marinade spooned over them as they cook. It may be necessary to do several batches. If so, transfer directly to your serving plate. They will cook very quickly and are easy to spoil by overcooking.

After 2 or 3 minutes over the heat (which should

be quite fierce), the prawns will start to shrivel in their shells and turn pinky white. Juices will collect in the shell. They should continue to cook until only the very centre area remains translucent, bluish and raw. Quickly turn them over and grill on the flesh side for no more than 1 minute.

When all the prawns are cooked and transferred to the serving dish, scatter with the parsley, tomato and onion. A little extra oil may be appropriate, lemon juice certainly is. Leave to cool while the flavours blend. Do not refrigerate.

Little **Tip**

■ **The leftover shells form the basis of an excellent fish broth.**

Gamberi e Fagioli
Prawns and Beans

One of those odd 'surf and turf' type food combinations, but not a wacky invention of post Nouvelle Cuisine nonsense. This dish seems to have developed traditionally in several regions simultaneously, notably Tuscany and the Veneto. The beans are the same as for Tonno e Fagioli (see opposite), the prawns are tiger prawns, briefly cooked in a strong court-bouillon, and the seasoning is provided by Gremolata (see page 125). Everything except the gremolata can be prepared in advance.

4 people
24 tiger prawns, headless but shell
    on (16–20 per 500 g count to
    your fishmonger)
500 g cooked cannellini beans (see
    page 104) or tinned
2 tbsp Gremolata (see page 125)
top-quality olive oil

For the court-bouillon:
1/2 bottle white wine
4 lime leaves (get from oriental
    stores)
1 carrot, peeled and cut into
    attractive rounds
1 onion, peeled and cut into rings
1 celery stick, stringed and
    finely sliced
sea salt
parsley stalks (from Gremolata)
20 black peppercorns

To make the court-bouillon, add 1 litre of water to the wine in a medium saucepan, then add the lime leaves and vegetables. Season very heavily with salt and add the parsley stalks and peppercorns. Bring to the boil and simmer for 30 minutes while you peel the prawns. Keep the prawn shells in your freezer and use them in Fish Broth (see page 186).

Bring the court-bouillon to a boil and drop the prawns in it. Turn off immediately, and tip out into a wide deep tray to cool as quickly as possible. Leave the prawns to cool completely in the liquid. Meanwhile, pick out the lime leaves, parsley and peppercorns.

To assemble the salad, drain 1 serving spoon of beans per person and put in a mixing bowl. Drain the prawns and the vegetables and add these to the bowl. Add the gremolata and a small amount of court-bouillon. Toss very gently and portion out on to small plates. Moisten each plate with a few drops of the oil. Possibly serve with lemon halves.

Tonno e Fagioli
Tuna and Beans

An old standby of trattorie around the world. A true larder dish, as everything comes out of a tin or a bottle. However, if you can be bothered to cook your own cannellini beans, the result is infinitely superior.

6 people
250 g leftover Baked Tuna (see
  page 152) or best-quality tinned
  tuna (Spanish, packed in olive oil,
  is the best and very expensive)
250 g cooked cannellini beans (see
  page 104) or tinned
juice of 1 lemon
a handful of parsley, chopped
salt and pepper
very good olive oil
1 red onion, peeled and sliced

If using tinned tuna open, drain and flake. If using tinned beans, open, drain and rinse very thoroughly, then drain well again.

Put the beans in a salad bowl. Add half the lemon juice then half the parsley. Season, then dress with enough oil to coat the beans lightly. (If you have just cooked the beans, dressing them warm adds a whole new dimension to this dish.)

Arrange the beans on a serving platter. Slice or flake the tuna and scatter on top. Scatter the red onions and the remaining parsley over. Drizzle with a little more oil. Do not make too far in advance.

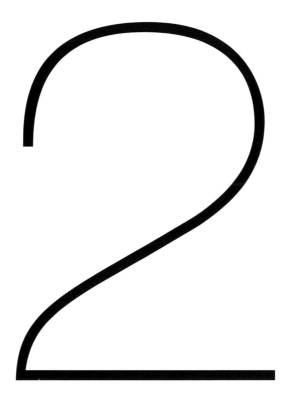

Zuppe e minestre

Soups and Broths All great cuisines have great soups, from delicate and sophisticated consommés to hearty virtual meals. The Italian taste for simplicity in food has produced some truly wonderful soups, far, far removed from the acidic tomato-ey diced vegetable travesty that minestrone frequently is here.

Minestrone Primavera
Spring Minestrone

This is an absolutely classic minestrone using seasonal vegetables, a pulse (in this case cannellini beans), a pasta (ditali) and finished with pesto. The method and sequence of cooking are fundamental: follow them step by step and the dish works. You can substitute different vegetables in different seasons. The pesto is not an authentic touch; it comes from the Nice region of France, which was originally part of the Kingdom of Savoy.

8–10 people
1 large onion, peeled
2 medium carrots, peeled
2 celery sticks, strings removed
6 courgettes, topped and tailed
12 medium asparagus stalks, peeled
1 small head broccoli
4 plum tomatoes, skinned and diced
1 kg peas in pod, podded
   (100 g frozen)
1 kg broad beans in pod, podded
   (100 g frozen)
500 g cooked cannellini beans
   (see page 104; tinned will do)
good olive oil
2 garlic cloves, peeled and minced
salt and pepper
300 g ditali
Pesto (see page 188)

Cut the onion, carrots, celery and courgettes into 5 mm dice. Keep them separate. Cut the asparagus stalks into 1 cm lengths. Peel the broccoli stems and dice; cut the heads into small florets. In a wide, heavy-bottomed pan or casserole heat 4 tbsp olive oil over a medium heat. Add the celery, carrot and onion and sweat for 10 minutes, stirring occasionally, until lightly coloured. This mixture of celery, carrot and onion is known as soffritto, and is the holy trinity of Italian cuisine.

Add the remaining vegetables and garlic, excluding the cannellini beans. Sweat for a further 10 minutes (you may need a little more oil). Season with salt and pepper, stir and add enough water to just cover the solids. Simmer until all the vegetables are tender (the carrots will be the judge of that).

Meanwhile blanch the ditali in boiling salted water for 4 minutes. Refresh in cold water and dress very lightly with olive oil to keep the pieces separate.

When the vegetables are tender, add the beans and pasta and simmer for 5 minutes. The soup is ready. Offer pesto for your guests to add to the soup.

Minestrone d'Estate

Summer Minestrone

This is an amalgam of summer vegetables cooked in vegetable stock with olive oil. The important ingredient is fresh borlotti beans (these are available from June onwards). The other distinguishing factor is that it includes lots of fresh tomato. I think it is delicious at room temperature.

This soup depends on two things for its effect. Firstly, the quality of the vegetables; be careful in selection, and be very careful to get the dicing right. If they are left too large it will make the soup coarse. The second is the stock; we have no garlic, chilli or pesto here to hide behind, just good vegetable broth.

8–10 people

1 kg fresh borlotti beans, podded
250 g runner beans, strings
    removed
4 medium bunches carrots, peeled
6 small summer turnips, scrubbed
12 new potatoes, scraped
6 medium courgettes, topped
    and tailed
6 ripe plum tomatoes, skinned
    and seeded
6 large spring onions, trimmed
1 kg spinach, washed
good olive oil
salt and pepper
1 litre Vegetable Broth (see page 187)

Prepare all the vegetables. Cook the borlotti for 30–40 minutes until tender, allow to cool in their liquor (this can be done in advance), then drain well as their cooking liquor becomes rather murky and would spoil the soup. Cut the runner beans diagonally into thin strips; they may benefit from a brief preliminary boiling – 3 minutes in salted water. Dice the carrots, turnips, new potatoes, courgettes and tomatoes. Keep them separate. Cut the spring onions into 2 cm lengths, and remove the stalks from the spinach before roughly chopping the leaves.

In a large pan heat 4 tbsp olive oil over a medium heat. Add all the vegetables except the spinach, borlotti and tomatoes. Season lightly and, stirring continuously, sweat until translucent, about 10 minutes. The potatoes sticking often indicates when this sweating process is done. Do not neglect this step, as the slowish cooking in the olive oil releases sugars and flavours from the vegetables which are lightly coloured. This is where quality flavour will come from.

Add the stock, turn the heat up, stir and bring to the boil. Turn the heat down again to medium and cook the soup somewhere between simmer and boil (slow boil to fast simmer) until the vegetables are done, about 30 minutes. Add the tomatoes, spinach and borlotti and cook for a further 10 minutes, stirring occasionally. Check the seasoning and serve.

Minestrone d'Autunno
Autumn Minestrone

Autumn in Italy means funghi porcini. Here we use the dried porcini (ceps). They come in various grades from very expensive large slices to a virtual powder.

8–10 people
2 onions, peeled
2 carrots, peeled
heart of 1 head celery
2 leeks, trimmed and washed
1 celeriac, peeled
200 g button mushrooms, washed
good olive oil
2 garlic cloves, peeled and minced
100 g dried ceps, diced and
    reconstituted in 1.5 litres warm
    water
300 g ditali, blanched and lightly oiled
truffle oil
Parmesan, freshly grated

Cut the onions, carrots, celery, leeks and celeriac into 5 mm dice. Keep them separate. Quarter and dice the button mushrooms.

In a large pan heat 4 tbsp olive oil and add the celery, carrots, onion and leek and sweat for 5 minutes. Add the celeriac, button mushrooms and garlic and sweat for 5 minutes more. Drain the ceps, reserving the liquid, but sieving it through a tea strainer. Add the ceps to the pan, toss and add their strained liquor. Stir and simmer over a medium heat for approximately 40 minutes until tender.

Purée half the soup, and re-mix with the unpuréed half. Add the pasta and bring back to a simmer. Stir until the pasta is tender, about 5 minutes.

To serve, ladle the hot soup into bowls, and pour a little truffle oil into each bowl. Parmesan is allowed.

■ Drain ceps by lifting them from the surface of their soaking liquid with your hands, a small sieve or a spider. If you pour them through a sieve, the grit that has just been soaked off them will be washed right back on. Examination of the soaking liquor before sieving will show how much grit there can be.

Minestrone d'Inverno
Winter Minestrone

A soup that is finished in the oven, and which is incredibly ribsticking, nourishing and delicious. The quantities given are large, so invite a lot of hungry friends, or save some for the next day. Italians show a penchant for eating their heartier soups as leftovers at room temperature. This may seem slightly unappetising, but believe me, one can acquire the taste. (Minestrone for breakfast?)

10 people
250 g dried broad beans,
    soaked overnight
1 smoked gammon hock (knuckle)

To cook the beans, drain and rinse them, and put in a large pan with the ham hock and approximately twice their volume of water. Bring to the boil, drain and discard the water. Replace with fresh cold water in the same proportion

2 bay leaves, 1 sprig rosemary, 1
    sprig thyme, tied into a bouquet
    garni
2 carrots, peeled
2 celery sticks, strung
2 onions, peeled
1 large turnip
2 large potatoes, peeled
500 g winter greens (if possible,
    cavolo nero), or outer leaves of
    Savoy cabbage
2 garlic cloves, peeled
4 small dried chillies
good olive oil
Parmesan, freshly grated
top-quality, new-season olive oil

and return to the boil. Turn the heat down low and skim thoroughly. Add the bouquet garni and simmer until the beans are tender, between 1 and 2 hours, depending on the age of the beans (the older the drier, the longer to cook). Allow to cool in their liquor. Keep the bouquet garni. This part is the protein of the dish, the solid heart, now for the flavours.

To cook the soup, preheat the oven to 150°C/300°F/ Gas 2. Cut the carrots, celery, onions, turnip and potatoes into 5 mm dice, keeping the potatoes separate. Cut out the stalks of the greens then roll up the leaves into a cylinder and slice finely across. Pulverise the garlic and chillies in a spice blender or in a mortar and pestle.

Put the diced vegetables, apart from the potatoes, in an ovenproof casserole with 3 tbsp of the good olive oil. Sweat over a low heat for 10 minutes, then add the garlic and chilli mix and the potato dice. Toss, then add the cooking liquor from the beans and ham plus the bouquet garni, as well as the beans. Shred the cooked ham and add along with the ham bones. Add enough water to cover the solids and stir. Continue simmering while you add all these ingredients.

Cover the casserole and bake in the preheated oven for 1 hour. After this time check the soup is not completely solid. Add a little water if necessary, and the shredded greens. Stir, re-cover and return to the oven for 30 minutes.

Remove from the oven and leave in a safe place, lid on, to cool down (it will be volcanically hot).

Serve directly from the casserole, opening it at the table. Offer grated Parmesan and new-season olive oil.

Minestrone di Razza
Skate Minestrone

A wonderful soup from a restaurant oddly called 'Paris', situated in Trastavere, and one of Rome's many excellent Jewish restaurants. You will need the Fish Broth (see page 186) for this recipe. Salt cod can be substituted for the skate, or any other flaky white fish. You will also need to make Roullle, a French import probably offered as a sop to the restaurant's name as all the rest of their food remains resolutely Roman.

6–8 people
2 carrots, peeled and cut into
 5 mm dice
2 celery sticks, stringed and cut into
 5 mm dice
1 onion, peeled and cut into
 5 mm dice
1 leek (optional), cut into 5 mm
 dice and washed thoroughly
100 g tinned tomato pieces
6 tbsp good olive oil
1.5 litres Fish Broth (see page 186)
salt and pepper
1 kg skate wing, skinned, boned
 and cut into large bite-sized strips
Rouille (see page 187)
Crostini (see page 102)
Parmesan, freshly and coarsely
 grated

Put all the vegetables except the tomatoes in a large pan with the olive oil and sweat over a medium flame for 10 minutes. Add the tomato and broth, then simmer until the vegetables are very tender, about 40 minutes. The soup can be held at this point, as the skate is only poached in it just before serving.

Bring the minestrone back to the boil (if left to cool), and check the seasoning. Drop the skate bits in and stir gently. Simmer for 5 minutes then serve with the rouille, crostini and Parmesan separately like a soupe de poissons.

■ Demand that your fishmonger skins and bones the skate for you. The boiling itself is easy, but the skinning is definitely a black art, and best left to skilled practitioners.

Ribollita

Much complicated nonsense is talked about this Tuscan soup. As its name implies, it is simply a re-boiled soup or, more accurately, re-boiled minestrone. Any bean-based minestrone will do, but the Winter Minestrone recipe is definitely a good candidate. Be careful, as it remains very hot for 20 minutes or so out of the oven. With it, drink cheap, cheerful and abundant Sangiovese (Chianti).

8–10 people
2 litres Winter Minestrone (see
 overleaf), omitting the greens
8 good slices stale bread (sliced
 white will not do)

Preheat the oven to 200°C/400°F/Gas 6.

Purée half the minestrone, and combine with the unpuréed half. Mix with the shredded cavolo nero. Put a little in an ovenproof casserole then arrange slices of stale bread to cover the base, slightly overlapping them.

200 g cavolo nero, winter greens
or outer leaves of Savoy
cabbage, shredded
100 g Parmesan, freshly grated
good olive oil

Add a little more minestrone, then another layer of bread and the rest of the minestrone. Sprinkle the top with a little Parmesan and a little oil. Bake uncovered in the preheated oven for 40 minutes. Cover loosely if the top gets too brown.

Risi e Bisi
Rice and Peas

The Venetian dialect for rice and peas. Virtually every cuisine has a rice and peas dish: jambalaya in New Orleans, gohan in Japan, and Chinese fried rice with peas. This is not a risotto, but a pea and ham soup thickened to solidity by the rice. To be candid, the end result is not that different.

6–8 people
1.5 kg peas in pod
500 g carnaroli rice (for strict
authenticity, but arborio will do)
1.5 litres Chicken or Vegetable
Broth (see pages 186 or 187)
60 g butter
1 onion, peeled and very finely diced
100 g pancetta, cut into small
lardons
60 g Parmesan, freshly grated
1 handful parsley, chopped
salt and pepper

Pod the peas. Do not discard the pods, but instead string and chop them into small pieces, then boil for 20 minutes in the broth. Sieve, and discard the pods, but admire the strong pea flavour of the liquid.

Take a heavy casserole or pan and melt the butter over a medium heat. Add the onion and pancetta and sweat for 5 minutes. Add the peas and sweat for a further 5 minutes. Add all the broth and simmer for 10 minutes after returning to the boil.

Tip in the rice, stir, cover and continue simmering for 20 minutes. At this point the rice should be al dente, cooked but not soft, slightly resistant to the bite. Taste and wait for a minute or two; if you detect a chalky residue in your mouth, it's still underdone.

The risi e bisi at this point is still quite liquid. Add the Parmesan and parsley, stir, cover and leave to rest for 4 minutes. During this time the dish will solidify slightly. Check seasoning. Serve warm.

Little **Tip**

■ Mint can be very successfully substituted for parsley. For a vegetarian alternative, omit the pancetta and chicken broth and use vegetable broth instead.

ZUPPA DI PISELLI
Pea Soup

A delicious spring soup which appeals to the economically minded in that it utilises the pea pods. Serve chilled if you want.

6–8 people

1 kg fresh peas, podded, reserving
    the peas and pods separately

30 g butter

1 onion, 1 celery stick, 1 bunch mint
    and 1 carrot, all peeled, stringed,
    stalked and very finely diced into
    a soffritto

2 large potatoes, peeled and diced

salt and pepper

croûtons (sliced stale bread cut into
    1 cm dice and deep-fried, optional)

4 tbsp crème fraîche

a little hot paprika

Bring 2 litres water to a rolling boil. Blanch the peas for 8–10 minutes or until tender. Remove the peas and refresh in cold water, drain and dry, then reserve. Do not throw away the cooking water, it provides the liquid for the soup.

In a largish casserole or saucepan (how large? Answer: large enough to accommodate the ingredients), melt the butter, add the soffritto, and sweat for 10 minutes over a medium to low heat. Add the potato dice and sweat for a further 5 minutes, until they start to stick.

While the soffritto is sweating, string the pea pods, and chop them coarsely. Add to the soffritto and potato and toss. Add enough of the pea cooking water to barely cover the vegetables. Season and stir. Turn up the heat and boil until the potato dice disintegrate. Allow to cool for a few minutes off the heat. Purée this soup mix in a liquidiser. Pour it through a fine sieve, pressing hard to get everything through except the stringier bits of the pods. I tend to make my puréed vegetable soups rather thick and then add more water if necessary. Like salt, excess

water is difficult to remove from a dish.

To serve, reheat the soup with the peas in it, and check the seasoning. Serve with the croûtons and a spoonful of crème fraîche in each soup plate, and a very light dusting of hot paprika – more for colour contrast than taste.

Little **Tip**

■ Pea pods contain a shiny 'lining'. This is inedible (and certainly indigestible) in all but the youngest pods (such as mange touts). If you do use older pods, the pushing through a sieve is vital after the liquidising.

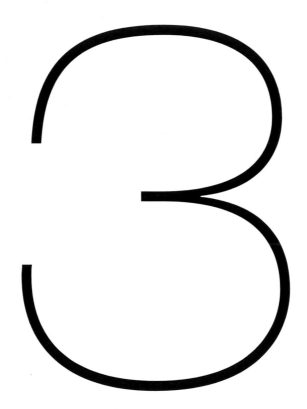

Pasta, Gnocchi e Crespelle

Pasta, Dumplings and Pancakes These categories are not related. We're grouping them here together because the recipes given are in the repertoire of the school.

PASTA ASCIUTTA | DRIED PASTA

There are an almost infinite number of types of pasta asciutta, especially if you include all the regional variations in names. Almost 90 per cent of the pasta eaten in Italy is dried, the remainder being home-made. Italians eat pasta every day; if they don't, they go 'cold turkey'. They have a whole vocabulary based around it. One of the nicest to me is 'butta la pasta', literally meaning to drop the pasta in the water. You hear burly middle-aged men shouting up to third and fourth floor apartment windows, 'Mamma, butta la pasta' ('Get lunch on the table, I'm home!'). A colander or sieve is known as a 'scuolopasta', as if they had nothing else to drain. Over the years at La Cacciata the guests each week have come up with a series of questions about pasta; week in week out, the exact same questions and misconceptions crop up. This indicates a gap between what cookbook writers assume the public knows on the subject, and the reality of the situation, which is one of surprising ignorance, so here is my 'Dried Pasta Seminar'.

What is pasta asciutta?
Semolina flour and water. It contains no egg and is fully dried.

What brands of pasta should I buy?
Da Cecco is a good all-round brand in pretty packaging. Nearly all Italian pasta is of good quality, the domestic market won't put up with less. Avoid pasta made anywhere else but Italy.

Why are some brands much more expensive?
These are either silly coloured designer pasta which I believe you can completely ignore as window dressing, or more interestingly 'pasta artisanale', literally 'craft made'. The large pasta companies dry their pasta in enormous ovens at 120°C for about 1 hour, producing a noodle that is in effect partially cooked. Cut a piece of commercial spaghetti and look at the cross section, the inside has a different colour and texture from the outside. The pasta artisanale is dried for up to 12 hours at 60°C producing a uniformity through the noodle. This difference coupled with the fact that small companies tend to buy better flour and use mineral water, simply means the pasta cooks better and has a superior texture, and in many ways texture is what pasta is all about. Good brands of pasta artisanale are Masseria and Latina, the latter just introduced into the English market. Pasta artisanale costs almost twice as much as pasta industrielle but is still a bargain.

How much pasta do I cook per person?
80 g–100 g. This is a perfectly good portion for pasta which should always be eaten as a first course. If you have pasta as a main course you will be hungry again within 2 hours: millions of Italians know this, they can't all be wrong. Pasta dishes feel and taste right as the beginning of a meal.

Clara Belcapo's Tagliatelle Aglio, Olio

How long do I cook it for?

Most types of dried pasta will cook perfectly well in under 10 minutes. The cooking times on British packaging are often grossly overstated. Spaghetti that has been stored too long and is over-dry may take longer and you might not want to eat the result (over-long here is measured in decades).

How much water do I cook it in?

A lot, between 500 ml and 1 litre per person, the more the better. The reason behind this is that the water should always be at a fiercely rolling boil before you 'butta la pasta'. The more water you have in proportion to pasta the quicker this water will return to the boil after the pasta is added. This means quick cooking and better textured pasta.

Do I salt the water?

Yes, lightly to taste unless you have dietetically sound reasons for avoiding salt.

Do I add oil to the water?

No. This is a trick used by restaurants to stop pre-cooked spaghetti from sticking together. As there is never any need to pre-cook pasta, this is redundant.

Is pasta fattening?

Yes, if you eat lots and are an idle bastard! Pasta is almost total carbohydrate, great fuel; marathon runners live on it, and any type of physical work or exercise will burn it off. Just walking a little will do the trick. Avoid eating too much if you have a sedentary existence.

When do I serve Parmesan?

In Britain we tend to assume that grated Parmesan is served with nearly every pasta dish. In fact, relatively few dishes call for cheese. Pasta with seafood never has it, the whole aglio, olio family ignore it, and tomato sauces sometimes do, sometimes don't. As a rule of thumb, if the sauce contains meat, butter or cream then Parmesan is required.

Can I use any shape of pasta with the same sauce?

You can, but I wouldn't advise it. I tend to stick to traditional combinations of shape and sauce. The Italians have been at this business for a very long time (long before Marco Polo) and have most aspects completely covered, including what constitutes the best combinations. When pasta is drained a certain amount of water clings to it, and some shapes retain more water than others. When this pasta is sauced the water combines, extends and in some cases emulsifies the sauce. A different shape would retain a different amount of water and produce a different taste.

What does 'al dente' mean?

It means 'to the tooth' and when applied to pasta it means a slight resistance to the bite, not half cooked, but keeping an interesting texture (over-cooked pasta is mushy and sloppy). Remember pasta continues to cook after draining and saucing. The only way to master this timing is to practise, make a lot of Spaghetti Aglio, Olio, and learn as you cook and eat.

Can I prepare pasta dishes in advance?

With the exception of baked pasta dishes such as lasagne, no pasta dish should be cooked ahead of time. The bloody stuff only takes a few minutes to cook, it is really fast convenience food. Bringing your pot of water to the boil is generally the most time-consuming part of the process. Sauces can be prepared in advance, but only cook and sauce the pasta at the last minute.

Do I need any special equipment?

Not really. A large pan is obvious, a largish colander is vital, a sieve and a spider are useful, and, if you are really serious, a pasta basket from a catering shop.

Spaghetti (Spaghettini) Aglio, Olio

Spaghetti (Spaghettini) with Garlic and Oil

This is a seminal pasta dish, in many ways the simplest of all. Master this one and you are well on the way to becoming an accomplished pasta cook.

6 people

500 g spaghetti or spaghettini
salt
5 tbsp good olive oil
4 small dried chillies (more if you're a
    vindaloo wallah), finely chopped
2 garlic cloves, peeled and crushed

Put 5 litres water on to boil. Put a colander in the sink. Warn your guests that food is imminent. This dish depends on speed of service for its quality. Salt the water. When boiling vigorously, add the pasta.

Immediately put a medium frying pan over a flame. Add the oil, chilli and garlic. The garlic may colour slightly, but must not burn – turn the heat down very low.

When the pasta is al dente, after about 8 minutes, drain through the colander, having reserved a small jug of the cooking water. Return the pasta quickly to the cooking pan, and place over a high flame. Immediately add the flavoured oil, toss and serve.

■ The cooking water was reserved because you may have over-drained the pasta. The success of this dish relies on an emulsion between the water and the oil thoroughly coating the pasta. If this doesn't happen, the pasta will be sitting in a pool of oil, so add a little of the water and heat vigorously for a few seconds.

Clara Belcapo's Variation

An Umbrian version using egg tagliatelle. Spinosi is the brand to go for here. Remember, the pasta will cook in 1 1/2-2 minutes. Add 1 finely chopped bay leaf, the leaves from a sprig of rosemary, finely chopped, and 6 finely chopped sage leaves to the oil with the chilli and garlic, and proceed as above.

Spaghettini con Vongole Veraci
Spaghettini with Clams

When the Italians sneer at '*stranieri*' (foreigners or barbarians) because they know nothing about food, they always pick on two particular sins. Firstly drinking cappuccino after 11 in the morning: to them to ask for cappuccino after dinner is like asking for shredded wheat as your dessert. Cappuccino is breakfast. Secondly, and even more serious, is putting Parmesan on Spaghettini con Vongole Veraci. Only an uncultured lout or a British tourist could do this.

This dish is simplicity itself – it just needs confidence and practice. It involves two processes: the cooking of spaghettini and the cooking of vongole veraci (palourde clams) in flavoured oil. The two are combined, parsley and a little of the cooking water is added, and bingo, a marvellous dish.

6 people
500 g spaghettini (thin spaghetti)
1.5 kg palourde clams
salt and pepper
1 tbsp good olive oil
2 tbsp Infused Oil (see page 187)
handful of fresh parsley, chopped

Little **Tip**

■ This recipe uses all the same techniques as aglio, olio (overleaf).

Put 5 litres water on to boil and salt lightly. Rinse the clams thoroughly under cold water for 1 hour. Discard any broken ones.

When the water is boiling, heat a large frying pan over a high heat. Add a little olive oil to this, and throw in the clams. Do not cover. At the same time drop the spaghettini in the boiling water and stir. Do not cover. The spaghettini will take 8 minutes, so have your colander ready in the sink. The clams will open at odd times. If you are being really fussy, remove the early openers (after 2 or 3 minutes), and set aside. The reason for this is that these early birds will overcook and fall out of their shells, leaving your guests with the extreme disappointment of empty shells.

When the spaghettini is done, drain it, reserving a little water in a jug. Return the pasta swiftly to the pan. Tip in the clams, return to the heat, and add the infused oil and parsley. Toss thoroughly and serve.

Spaghetti alla Genovese
Spaghetti with Pesto, Sliced Potatoes and Green Beans

A Ligurian dish that the Genoese insist must be made with plain dried pasta, never fresh, and certainly without eggs. Why they insist on this escapes me, but over the years I've noticed that Italians are quite good at pasta so I rarely ignore their advice, even if it seems pointless. The dish must also be made with home-made pesto. The inclusion of potatoes seems strange to non-Italians – starch upon starch, an anathema to many diets – but it works, the slices of potato absorbing any excess olive oil rendered out by the action of the spaghetti's heat on the pesto. They absorb the oil, and are themselves transformed. It all makes perfect sense when you get it in your mouth.

This is a good dish to show the basic steps of cooking pasta and to exemplify the gusto and confidence needed to succeed: a series of simple steps executed correctly in sequence and at speed.

6 people
500 g spaghetti
5 large new potatoes
150 g very fine French beans,
    topped and tailed
6 generous tbsp Pesto (see
    page 188)
salt and pepper

■ Don't muck about with the pesto
for this dish. It won't work with
coriander or mint, however
delicious these concoctions may
be in other contexts.

Prepare the pesto, potatoes and beans. These can be done in advance; the veg up to 1 day before, the pesto almost any time. Boil the potatoes in their skins in lightly salted water until tender, then drain well and slice thinly. Boil the beans in heavily salted, violently boiling water for 3 minutes, then drain, refresh in cold water and drain again.

Put 5 litres water on to boil and salt it lightly. Drop the pasta into the water and stir. Cook for 8 minutes then test.

Take your serving bowl and warm it up by ladling into it a litre of the pasta cooking water. Add the beans and potatoes to this water to heat through. Drain the veg, return to the serving bowl and add the pesto. Put a colander in the sink.

When the pasta is al dente, drain and reserve a small jug of the cooking water. Working quickly and carefully, remove the pan from the stove but leave the heat on. Drain the pasta in the colander, then return to the hot pan still dripping. Return the pan to the heat for 30 seconds to get very hot. Tip the pesto, bean and potato mix on to the spaghetti and toss. It will almost certainly be a little dry so add some of the reserved water and toss. Switch off the heat under the pan. Taste to check seasoning and adjust. One final toss and tip into the serving dish and out to your guests.

Conchiglie Primavera
Springtime Pasta Shells

This dish was shown to me five years ago at La Cacciata. I rushed back to Wandsworth and bored Richard Whittington, my colleague who was writing *Keep It Simple* with me at the time. 'We must put this in the book,' I urged, 'it's the best thing I've ever tasted, it's never been seen before out of Italy.' Richard nodded indulgently and advised me to watch some supermarket commercials then current. I did, and saw my wonderful new discovery being broadcast to millions. Crestfallen doesn't begin to describe it.

There is however a sub-text to the supermarket's advertising campaign. Take industrially made poor quality conchiglie, 6 unripe flavourless tomatoes, 100 g of nasty tasteless pasteurised plastic-clad ricotta, some overpriced feeble hot-house basil and a bog standard olive oil. Cook the pasta until it is as near al dente as inferior pasta will allow you to get, dice the tomatoes without peeling. Dress the pasta with table salt and black sneezing powder, the oil and the tomatoes and glop ricotta. Result, a scarcely edible dish.

To make this dish properly, you need to find good ingredients. Follow the simple instructions and enjoy; diverge, and disaster will follow.

6 people
500 g conchiglie
8 large, ripe, flavoursome plum
    tomatoes
1 bunch very fresh and pungent
    basil
150 g very fresh ricotta (see if you
    can find ricotta di bufala, pester
    your delicatessen)
top-quality olive oil
salt and pepper

The timing of this dish is almost as important as the freshness and quality of the ingredients.

1–2 hours in advance
Dip the tomatoes for exactly 1 minute in boiling water, then plunge into cold water. Drain and peel with a small knife. Chop the tomatoes in 1 cm pieces; you do not need to remove the seeds. Scrape the tomato pieces and their juices into a large bowl. Season generously with salt and pepper and a liberal slug of the olive oil. Break up the basil leaves and mix in. Leave covered in a cool place until needed. The salt will draw out the juices from the tomatoes and form a sauce.

30 minutes before serving
Put 5 litres of water on to boil, and lightly salt it. When the water is boiling vigorously, drop the pasta in and stir immediately to try and prevent it sticking to the pot. The pasta will take approximately 9–10 minutes to cook. Whilst it is cooking, do two things. Put a colander in the sink and mix the ricotta with the by now 'soupy' tomatoes in the bowl.

For some dishes dried pasta like conchiglie is drained when really rather undercooked because it will continue to cook as it is sauced – Spaghetti Aglio, Olio for example. Conchiglie Primavera is a different case as the sauce is raw (sugo crudo), and when the pasta and sauce are mixed the relatively large amount of cold ingredients lower the temperature of the pasta and arrest the cooking. Consequently the pasta must be drained at the correct point, when truly al dente, then sauced very quickly and served with dispatch.

Serving

Before draining the pasta, reserve a small jug of cooking water. Pour the rest of the pasta water carefully through the colander (carefully, because even steam can scald). Working quickly, transfer the drained pasta back to the cooking pot. Tip in the tomato and ricotta mix and thoroughly toss again, working speedily. Either serve at table or portion up in the kitchen. Do *not* add Parmesan to the dish.

Little **Tips**

■ Do not be tempted to try this dish with mozzarella. Take my word, it doesn't work. In fact don't muck about with this recipe at all, it's perfect as it is.

■ For Penne con Sugo Crudo (with raw tomato sauce), follow the above recipe exactly but omit the ricotta and be more generous with olive oil.

Penne con Salsicce
Pasta Quills with Sausages

Italian sausages are wonderful as a meal (see page 138) but crumbled up and cooked with onions and a tomato sauce, make a hearty and deeply satisfying pasta sauce.

6 people
500 g penne rigate
400 g Italian sausages, spicy if possible
6 tbsp good olive oil
1 large onion, peeled and sliced into rings
500 ml Rich Tomato Sauce (see page 189)
salt and pepper

Heat half the olive oil in a saucepan and sweat the onion rings over a medium heat. They should collapse and colour lightly. This takes half an hour or so, and only needs the occasional stir. While this is cooking make the tomato sauce if you don't have any ready. Again while the onions are simmering, peel the sausages. This is done by running them under a cold tap then gently but firmly pulling off the skins. Chop into bite-sized pieces.

Put the remaining oil into a large non-stick frying pan and brown the sausage pieces. It doesn't matter if they break up or stick, simply chisel them free. When they are brown add the by now collapsed onions and the tomato sauce. Simmer together for 20 minutes. The sauce is now ready. It can be cooled and stored for up to 3 days.

Put 5 litres lightly salted water on to boil, half an hour before you wish to eat. Reheat the sauce in a large pan (and heat a serving bowl if using one). Put a colander into the sink. Boil the pasta for 8–9 minutes and check if done. Drain and add to the sauce. Toss thoroughly and serve. No Parmesan is needed.

Penne con Sugo di Pomodoro, Melanzane e Ricotta Salata
Penne with Rich Tomato Sauce, Aubergine and Salted Ricotta

This was served to me in a scruffy Sicilian trattoria close to the Vatican. The owner, cook and waiter was a woman with so vast a bosom that she couldn't get an apron over it. Instead she used a tablecloth tied above her *poitrine*. **Awesome. She told us exactly what to eat and we ate it.**

You will need a baby mouli-legumes to do this dish.

6 people

500 g penne rigate

2 large aubergines

150 g salted ricotta (you won't
   be able to find it, so buy good-
   quality feta)

For the rich Sicilian tomato sauce

500 g tinned tomato pieces

1 onion, peeled and finely diced

good olive oil

2 small dried chillies, minced

2 garlic cloves, peeled and minced

6 anchovy fillets, diced

a little sugar

10 black olives, stoned and very
   finely chopped

a handful of parsley, chopped

salt and pepper

■ This dish is very flexible in terms of
the type of pasta you use. Macaroni
may well be more authentic, but
cavatelli (they resemble earwigs) or
casarecci (squiggly worms) are
eminently suitable. They require a
couple more minutes' cooking.

To make the sauce, sauté the onion in 1 tbsp oil with the chilli and garlic until starting to colour. Add the tomatoes, stir and simmer for 10 minutes, then add the anchovies and a little sugar. Simmer this mixture, stirring occasionally, until reduced by half, about 30 minutes. Take off the heat, and stir in the olives, parsley and a little more oil. The sauce is ready. Check the seasoning and adjust if necessary. The sauce can be stored in the fridge for several days.

You can also prepare the aubergines at the same time as the tomato sauce. Slice the aubergines 5 mm thick lengthways. Lightly brush with olive oil, and season. Cook in a large frying pan dry for 5 minutes per side. You may need to do this in several batches. Lay out on a lightly oiled baking sheet in a single layer.

Preheat the oven to 120°C/250°F/Gas 1/2.

Put 5 litres slightly salted water on to boil half an hour before you wish to eat. Heat six soup plates in the oven, and put the aubergines in to heat up 15 minutes before time. Reheat the sauce, but be careful, it will catch and burn. Break the feta up and pack into the baby mouli. Boil the pasta for 8–9 minutes then taste. If done, drain in a colander, reserving a little of the pasta liquid in a jug. Return the pasta to the hot pan and add the hot sauce. Toss thoroughly, then portion out into the warmed soup plates. Put two slices of hot aubergine on top then, working quickly, mouli the cheese over each dish producing little white squiggles which partially melt on to the aubergine and sauce. Serve quickly.

PASTA ALL'UOVO
EGG PASTA

As a halfway stage between pasta asciutta and home-made or fresh pasta we have pasta all'uovo, which is made with semolina flour like spaghetti but incorporates eggs. It comes in a variety of shapes but is best as tagliatelle or fettucine. Like pasta asciutta, it is better from small 'artisanale' producers. A memorably good one is the firm of Spinosi from the Marche. This type of noodle has a more robust texture than home-made, and also has some of the keeping qualities of other dried pasta. The coloured varieties are in my opinion to be avoided. Always use the plain pasta; if you want colour and taste use the sauce to supply them.

Tagliatelle con Burro e Parmigiano
Egg Noodles with Parmesan and Butter

The most basic of all North Italian pasta dishes, and one of the most satisfying. Again it's a master recipe in terms of the techniques and problems involved.

6 people
500 g good-quality tagliatelle all'uova
salt and pepper
75 g butter
75 g Parmesan, freshly grated

Bring 5 litres of water to the boil and add salt. Put a colander in the sink. Cook the noodles – they will only take a couple of minutes – then drain in the colander and return to the pan. Place the pan back on a low flame, add the butter and Parmesan and toss thoroughly. Adjust the seasoning (coarsely grated black pepper is rather nice in this dish) and serve.

Little **Tip**

■ Reserve a jug of the pasta cooking water, and add a little if the pasta seems dry or the butter looks greasy.

Tagliatelle con Tartufo Bianco
Tagliatelle with White Truffle

If you can afford it and can find them you must try white truffles from Piedmont. You will need about 10 g per serving, and a second mortgage. They are just simply sliced very thinly over the tagliatelle described above.

Tagliatelle con Tartufo d'Umbria
Tagliatelle with Umbrian Summer Truffle

As above, but grate a frozen Umbrian summer truffle through the Parmesan holes of your grater directly on to the plates of noodles.

PASTA FRESCA
FRESH PASTA

Given the quality of manufactured egg pasta discussed earlier, it is really not necessary to make your own. Not necessary, true, but it can be fun if you like working with your hands and are not excessively preoccupied with fast food. Below are some recipes which require home-made pasta; they will not work without.

During the week's course at La Cacciata the guests make fresh hand-made pasta twice. The first session is to make lasagne or pappardelle. The second, which is always on Friday, the last night, is to make ravioli, usually with a stuffing of ricotta and Swiss chard. The whole group of guests join in, squabbling cheerfully about who is having too long a go on the rolling machine or whose ravioli are the best. They are enjoying themselves. The two hand-made pasta dishes are regarded as the best of the week; this is not necessarily true, of course, but is a reflection of the involvement and enjoyment shown by the cooks. Yes, these are not dishes to knock up in a hurry, but they reflect a slower pace, an interest in the craft, and a pride in what you do. Get your cuticles covered in flour, and have a go!

If you are going to make fresh pasta you will have to find the right ingredients, and you will also need a pasta machine. The basic roller type is just fine and fixes on to table tops with a G clamp. (Some modern kitchen units don't have a projecting top so the G clamp cannot fix on them.) You will need the following equipment and ingredients. The amount of dough made is enough for 8 people. Shaped pasta can be dried and stored.

Ingredients
Italian type 00 flour
Italian fine semola dura (hard fine
    semolina, French won't do)
good-quality eggs, but the
    pasteurised eggs now
    available from supermarkets
    are very effective

Equipment
1 pasta rolling machine (lots of people
    have them rusting in cupboards
    since their weddings)
1 ravioli cutter (crimped wheel on a handle)
1 pastry brush
1 tray for storing the finished pasta.
    Wickerwork is particularly effective as it
    allows air to circulate under the pasta
    and keep it dry. Bakers' trays are very
    good and handsome, otherwise use a
    normal laminated or plastic tray.

You will also need a large work space, the
day's newspaper and approximately 2 hours.

Regular Pasta Dough

The best method of working this pasta dough is by hand, but this requires strength, determination, stamina and a sense of humour. A combination of machine and hand will do nicely. The most effective machine is a food mixer with a dough hook; failing that, a food processor, but this is a very poor second best as it rather brutalises the dough where the hook stretches and kneads it.

250 g type 00 flour
250 g semola dura (hard fine
    semolina)
300 g pasteurised egg or
    6 eggs, no. 3

Combine all the ingredients in the mixer. Run at low speed until the dough forms a ball and begins to come away from the sides of the bowl. If too wet add a little 00 flour; if too dry a few drops of water.

Turn out on to a floured surface and knead the dough by pushing it with the heel of your hand, stretching it away from you, and then pulling it back. Turn through a quarter circle and repeat. It needs 100 kneads, or as near as dammit. You should have an elastic ball of dough. Wrap it in clingfilm and refrigerate for 1 hour or up to 4 hours, but no longer, or the dough will oxidise and develop little black dots.

Hideously Expensive and Rich Pasta Dough

To quote Gary Rhodes, this is the business.

250 g type 00 flour
250 g semola dura (hard fine
    semolina)
400 g egg yolks (about 16 no. 3)
2 whole eggs

Proceed as for the previous pasta. This is much harder to work and knead, but the finished product is well worth the labour and considerable expense. This dough keeps longer than the previous recipe, up to overnight.

Rolling Out Fresh Pasta

Divide the dough into four balls. Assemble the pasta machine. Dust the work surface with 00 flour. Have a container of semola ready, and lightly dust the storage tray with it.

Flatten the first ball out into a disc 1 cm thick, then open the pasta machine to its widest setting and feed the disc through the rollers. Fold in two lengthways. Narrow the rollers one setting and repeat. Keep doing this until you reach the narrowest setting. By this time the pasta may be unmanageably long – simply cut it. It should be thin enough to read a medium-sized newspaper headline through, over-thick pasta is a disaster! If anything goes wrong during the rolling process simply fold back and repeat. The re-rolling is an extra kneading, and in general the more times it is kneaded the better.

You now have a long oblong of pasta suitable for your selected dish. Simply cut, stuff or shape, according to the recipe. When this is done place the cut pasta in the container of semola to dust it, and transfer to the storage tray. Freshly made pasta sticks together; the semola keeps it separate.

When you have finished the first pasta ball, open the machine to its widest setting again, flatten another ball, and repeat the whole process.

■ There are a number of small things that can go wrong, most of which are curable by patience and persistence. Over-wet pasta will need careful handling and drying; over-dry dough will just be very hard work but you will have an excellent product at the end. After two or three attempts you will be nearly expert. It is just a question of practice and observation.

Pappardelle

Broad hand-made noodles from Tuscany, traditionally paired with hare, but not by me. I find hares altogether too endearing.

Make the Rich Pasta Dough and roll out as directed. With a crinkle cutter (ravioli cutter), cut noodles approximately 15 cm long and 2 cm wide. Individually dust them with semola and lay on the tray. The amount of dough given will be enough for ten people, but it keeps well if you leave it to dry overnight (cake racks are very good for drying small quantities).

I serve pappardelle with a classic Tuscan rabbit and sage sauce (see page 142).

Garganelle

A very good if labour-intensive pasta.

Make the Rich Pasta Dough and roll out. You also need a round pen and a large tooth comb.

Cut the pasta into 2 or 3 cm squares. Roll a square round the pen whilst pressing on the comb (preferably a clean one). You do this in a diamond shape i.e. – start with a point of the square rather than a straight edge. You will now have one ribbed roll of fresh pasta with nib type pointy ends. Repeat this procedure until the pasta is used up. This process seems slow but dexterity equals speed. You may also find that it will be better to only prepare twenty or so squares at a time as they may dry out and be unrollable.

When freshly made the garganelle will cook in a minute or so. When dried they will take a little longer.

Possible sauces are given on the following pages.

SAUCES FOR HOMEMADE PASTA

The following three sauces are delicious with egg tagliatelle, but if you really want a spectacular dish, make the Garganelle (see overleaf), and use instead.

Salsa d'Asparagi

Asparagus Sauce

To me asparagus is a true rite of spring: it cheers me up, and the clean flavour presages finer weather.

6 people

300 g asparagus spears
250–500 ml Vegetable Broth
    (see page 186)
salt
90 g butter
1/2 onion, peeled and very
    finely diced
60 g Parmesan, freshly grated

Peel and trim the asparagus, getting rid of the woody bits, then wash it thoroughly to get rid of sand. If using sprue, i.e. very thin asparagus, just trim the woody white ends; this asparagus probably has the best flavour for this dish. Keep the peelings and trimmings. Chop the asparagus into 2 cm lengths (5 cm for sprue). Boil the vegetable broth with the asparagus peelings and trimmings for 15–20 minutes to infuse, then sieve. Keep the broth hot and discard the solids.

Melt half the butter in a wide pan over a medium heat. Add the onion and asparagus and sweat for 3–4 minutes. Add the broth and turn up the heat to a boil. Cook for 10 minutes until the asparagus is very tender and the broth has nearly evaporated.

Meanwhile cook the pasta (ideally Garganelle, see overleaf), drain and add to the asparagus sauce. Add the remaining butter and the Parmesan, then toss again over a medium heat. Serve immediately.

Salsa di Piselli e Pancetta

Pea and Pancetta Sauce

This is an utterly classic combination, and crops up all over the world – pea and ham soup, Chinese fried rice, petits pois à la française. Obviously a good thing!

6 people

1 kg peas in pod
120 g pancetta, cut into 5 mm dice
500 ml Vegetable Broth (see page 186)
75 g butter
1/2 onion, peeled and very finely diced
salt and pepper
60 g Parmesan, freshly grated

Pod the peas. String and chop the pods, then boil in the vegetable broth for 20 minutes. Sieve and keep warm. Discard the solids.

Melt 60 g of the butter in a saucepan, add the onion and pancetta, and sweat for 10 minutes. The pancetta should be translucent. Add the peas, and sweat for a further 10 minutes. Add a little of the broth and simmer over a medium heat for a minimum of 20 minutes, by which time the liquid should have reduced considerably. The pancetta should be very tender. Big peas will take up to 40 minutes. The sauce can be made in advance.

Cook your pasta and drain. Return to the pan, and add the hot sauce, the remaining butter and the grated Parmesan. Season with freshly grated black pepper (this dish likes pepper), and possibly a little salt.

Salsa di Funghi Porcini e Tartufo
Cep and Truffle Relish

This is wonderful on Crostini (see page 102). It also makes an excellent sauce for spaghetti or tagliatelle. Simply cook the pasta, drain and return to the pan. Spoon in 1 dsp relish per person and generous grated Parmesan. Toss and serve. It is exceptionally delicious on the Salad of Roasted Vegetables on page 36.

100 g dried funghi porcini, soaked in 300 ml warm water
100 g summer truffles (frozen are good)
1 onion, peeled and very finely diced
20 ml good olive oil
salt and pepper
20 ml truffle oil

In a wide saucepan over a low heat sweat the diced onion in the olive oil. It must cook slowly and not brown, approximately 10–15 minutes.

While this is cooking carefully lift out the ceps from their water – use your fingers or a spider. This ensures that the inevitable grit remains behind in the water. Pat dry and dice, then add to the onions and continue to sweat together for 10 minutes further. During this time carefully strain the cep soaking water through a coffee filter or fine tea strainer. When the cep and onion mix has had the 10 minutes, add the cep liquor and turn the heat up to medium. Cook until the cep water is nearly completely evaporated. Set aside to cool.

Clean and sterilise a 450 g jar (dishwashers are good for this!).

Grate the truffles (straight from the freezer if frozen) through the same aperture of the grater as you would Parmesan, directly over the cooked cep and onion mix. Stir, taste and season, then add half the truffle oil. Using a rubber spatula, transfer this mixture to the jar. Pat down in the jar, wiping the edges inside the glass with a clean cloth. Top up the jar with the remaining truffle oil: the layer of truffle oil should cover the relish completely. Keep in the fridge; if unopened, almost indefinitely.

To use the relish, stir some more truffle oil into it.

LASAGNE DI BIETOLE
Swiss Chard Lasagne

To make this dish properly you really need to make fresh pasta. 'No-need-to-boil lasagne' sheets are an excellent product and fine for conventional uses, but in this one the pasta forms a crisp crust on top and only fresh dough will achieve this. You will need a lasagne dish, i.e. a deep heatproof rectangular dish: ceramic or earthenware dishes produce a better result than metal ones.

10 people

1 recipe Regular Pasta Dough

    (see page 74)

1 recipe Béchamel Sauce

    (see page 189)

salt and pepper

semola duro

150 g butter

150 g Parmesan, freshly grated

150 g Fontina cheese

nutmeg

2 bunches Swiss chard or 2 kg big-

    leaf spinach (both need destalking)

The 500 g packets of pre-made salsa besciamella available in Italian delicatessens are really rather good; you will need two packets for this recipe. You will also need a buttered lasagne dish about 25 x 55 cm and 5 cm deep.

Make the pasta dough a minimum of 1 hour before use.

Bring a large pan of boiling water to a boil, add some salt and prepare a bowl of cold water. While this is coming to the boil, roll out the pasta. Divide the dough into four and pass through rollers. When rolled through the narrowest setting, cut the pasta strips into 10 cm rectangles. Dust with semola and lay aside until you have prepared all the pasta dough. By this time the water should be boiling furiously. Individually drop the lasagne sheets in, doing them in two batches. They need 3 minutes' cooking, then fish them out with a spider and plunge into the cold water to refresh. Drain and pat dry with kitchen paper and lay out, slightly

overlapping, round a tray. Do not stack too high or they will stick together.

Heat up the béchamel sauce carefully (it has a strong tendency to scorch). Off the heat add one-third of the butter and the cheeses. Check the seasoning then grate in a little nutmeg. While you are doing this return the pasta water to a rolling boil and prepare a fresh basin of cold water. Add more salt to the pasta water. Blanch the chard or spinach for 1 minute, pushing it under the surface of the water with the spider. Then drain and refresh in the cold water. Drain as soon as it is cold and squeeze out as much water as possible. Now gently pull the squeezed balls of greens apart so you can find individual leaves. Put on a tray in a similar manner to the drained pasta.

Line the buttered lasagne dish with the sheets of pasta, first the base, then slightly overlapping the sides. Arrange the sides so the sheets hang over the edge of the dish. Now ladle in approximately one-quarter of the cheesy béchamel sauce. Cover this with chard leaves, again approximately one-quarter of them, then a layer of pasta, just enough to cover the chard. Repeat the béchamel, then the greens and then the pasta. Do this process two more times ensuring that you save at least 8 good sheets of pasta for the top. Arrange these carefully and then fold over the flaps of overhanging pasta from the sides. The dish can now be cooled and

kept refrigerated for up to one day.

To reheat the lasagne, preheat the oven to 200°C/400°F/Gas 6. Dot the lasagne with the remaining butter and put it into the oven to bake for 25 minutes. The béchamel should start to bubble and seep through the pasta crust which should be crisp and golden brown. If the top crust browns too much before the béchamel is hot turn the oven down to 150°C/300°F/Gas 2, cover loosely and then continue. Serve in the dish at the table, allowing 5 minutes for it to cool down a little.

RAVIOLI, TORTELLONI AND AGNOLOTTI

Three names for the same dish from the same region of Italy: Emilia Romagna, home of Parmesan, Parma ham, Gorgonzola and Bolognese sauce. Italians regard any food produced more than 10 km from their birthplace as foreign, so even localised specialities can arrive under a bewildering array of names. Don't try to sort all these names out; try to cook them all and wonder at the marvels of fresh pasta cooking from the heartland of Italian gastronomy. From here on I will refer to the dishes as ravioli, but I wish to point out that these recipes bear no resemblance to the rather fatuous overstuffed pillows now being offered in Michelin-starred restaurants. These blobs usually filled with over-processed mousses of seafood are not pasta dishes in that they reduce the pasta itself to an incidental ingredient. I've said it before and will again: the point of a pasta dish is the pasta itself, any other part of the dish is mere flavouring. Nor do these ravioli bear much resemblance to the small meat-filled pasta envelopes of southern Italy, delicious though many of these are.

Don't worry if your pasta looks distinctly unprofessional. Why go to all the trouble of making your own ravioli if they look so perfect that your guests assume you bought them!

■ All three of these recipes are sauced with butter. If you find this too rich, try substituting a little warmed very good olive oil poured moderately over the freshly boiled ravioli. I couldn't believe this would work when first offered it in Umbria but it does, and produces a lighter and healthier, but to my mind slightly inferior, result.

Assembling the Ravioli

The Dough

Generally the richer the dough, the better the ravioli. The recipe given on page 74 is near ideal. You should make the dough between 1 and 12 hours ahead, and keep it in the fridge wrapped in clingfilm.

Equipment

You will need a pasta machine. The small hand-cranked roller machines beloved of wedding-present lists are ideal – Imperia is a particularly good brand. Do not buy the ravioli attachment, it is useless for this dish. These pasta machines fix on the projecting top of a table, they often will not clamp on modern kitchen units. I consider a largish table essential for this procedure because you really do need a lot of space. You will also need a tray for the assembled ravioli, a pastry brush, a small bowl and, most important, a ravioli or crinkle-edged pastry cutter (do not buy the wooden ones, they are worse than useless).

Roll out the dough as described on page 74, but only prepare two strips of thin dough, approximately 1 metre long and 12 cm wide at a time, as they will dry out quickly. Lay these on the lightly floured table.

With a teaspoon form little balls of the stuffing and arrange in a row along the leading edge of the nearest pasta strip. These balls should be 1 cm in from the edge and 1 cm apart. They should not be positioned more than halfway across the width of the pasta sheet as the bare half is going to fold over and

8–10 people (depending on greed)

1 recipe of the chosen stuffing
(see pages 82-4)

1 recipe Rich Pasta Dough (see
page 74)

type 00 flour in a dredger/shaker

1 egg, beaten lightly in a small bowl

semola dura in a wideish bowl

form the top. Before you do this lightly moisten the pasta in front of the stuffing balls and between them with the beaten egg. (Careful the pastry brush isn't shedding its bristles – they often do.) While this egg wash is still wet, fold over the back half of the pasta, and press down between the stuffing balls to squeeze out the excess air. After sealing between the balls

press the front seam. Now, using the ravioli cutter, trim neatly along the front of the pasta to leave a 5 mm border of pasta between the by-now covered stuffing and the edge. This done, cut between each little covered mound of stuffing. When they are all cut, pick up individually and check that the seals on the three crinkled edges are tight. You do this by running your thumb and forefinger round and pressing. Drop these beautiful ravioli in the bowl of semola and dust thoroughly. Lightly dust the tray with semola and carefully place the little pasta envelopes on this in a single layer.

Repeat with the dozen or so ravioli made so far. Now repeat this whole performance with the other sheet of dough. Arrange the ravioli in very neat rows on the tray, try not to rest them on each other and as you get further on in your production do not double stack, find another tray instead. However dry you have made the stuffing it will still partially saturate the pasta under it, and stacking two ravioli on top of one another will guarantee two ruined ravioli.

So far you have only processed one-quarter of the dough. Carry on regardless – if you run out of stuffing before pasta simply roll the rest out as tagliatelle. If you run out of pasta it means you are using too much stuffing. One slightly more than level teaspoon in a ball is about right.

Little **Tips**

- **Don't over fill. If the filling is still wet, form balls
and then roll in grated Parmesan (they look like little
fancy cakes rolled in coconut).**

    **Don't worry if the first batches look a little rough,
this is a manual task and practice makes perfect.**

    The dusting with semola is very, very important.

Cooking the Ravioli

4 people

24–32 ravioli
salt
100 g butter
1/2 tsp cracked black pepper
12 sage leaves
4 level tbsp grated Parmesan

Bring 6 litres of water to a boil and salt it. In a separate large pan over a low heat melt the butter and add the black pepper and sage leaves to infuse. Drop 6–8 ravioli per person into the water. ('Butta la pasta'.)

Some authorities say that ravioli are ready when they float. This is nonsense, my home-made ones always contain pockets of air and bob engagingly immediately on hitting the water. The ravioli will take about 5 minutes but after 4 remove one and snip off a corner (where the pasta is double thickness and therefore taking longest to cook) to taste and check.

As soon as it is cooked, remove from the pan with a spider and transfer, still dripping, to the butter pan. Turn the heat up under the butter pan and add the Parmesan. Stir and toss gently until the butter, Parmesan and residual water amalgamate to form a coating sauce. Serve immediately. Any ravioli not served can be frozen.

STUFFINGS FOR RAVIOLI

A trio of fillings or stuffings for home-made ravioli.

Spinach or Swiss Chard Ravioli Stuffing

This is an adaptation of the Gnocchi recipe on page 90. Please glance at that to find out about cooking and drying the spinach. It is important that as much water as possible is extracted.

6–8 people

200 g spinach, cooked and
    squeezed (dry weight)
100 g ricotta cheese
50 g Parmesan, freshly grated
salt and pepper
freshly grated nutmeg

Hand chop the spinach and place in a large mixing bowl. Add the broken-up ricotta and the Parmesan. Season generously and add the nutmeg to taste. Mix thoroughly by hand. A food processor does not do this dish properly, it purées and homogenises the stuffing. Refrigerate until needed.

Pumpkin Ravioli Stuffing

I personally find the original for this dish rather bizarrely sweet, and in Britain substitute butternut squash for pumpkin. The other enemy of this dish is moisture – squashes are extremely watery, and if this is retained in the ravioli stuffing, it will soak into the pasta and give the envelopes a soggy bottom.

6–8 people

1 kg butternut squash
4 amaretti biscuits
2 tbsp drained Mostarda di
    Cremona (2–3 pieces),
    coarsely chopped
stale bread, toasted and ground
    for breadcrumbs
100 g Parmesan, freshly grated
salt and pepper
freshly grated nutmeg

Preheat the oven to 160°C/325°F/Gas 3.

Put the butternut squash into a roasting dish and bake for 1 1/2 hours until very tender and collapsed. Allow to cool, cut in half and remove seeds and skin. Put the flesh of the squash into a dry wide pan (a frying pan), and cook over a medium heat, stirring occasionally, until it has dried out and reduced its volume by half. Be careful on two points. Firstly, the squash must not stick and burn. Secondly, as the squash flesh breaks up, it will form a coarse purée; as this concentrates it begins to imitate those large bubbles that rise out of volcanic mud pools in nature documentaries. These bubbles are quite capable of popping viciously and spraying you with very hot squash pulp, so if those pustules are forming, turn down the heat and stir.

When you have concentrated the squash pulp (this takes nearly an hour), tip it into a food processor with the amaretti and mustard fruits. Process a little then pour out into a large mixing bowl and add a handful of breadcrumbs and an equivalent amount of cheese. Mix and taste. Now the hard part – I can give you no hard and fast amounts – you will need more crumbs to absorb the liquid but too much will ruin the taste of the stuffing, and you will certainly need more Parmesan, lots of seasoning (salt, pepper and nutmeg), perhaps more amaretti, perhaps more Mostarda di Cremona. Only you can decide, but bear in mind two things, the resulting mix should be capable of holding its shape and should not be too sweet (I stress *too* as it is a sweet mixture). Remember this is a stuffing, so add plenty of seasoning.

When you are happy, transfer to a clean container and refrigerate for up to 2 days. This mix also freezes quite well. Incidentally, half-cooked assembled ravioli freeze well, and are best reheated by 1 minute in boiling water from frozen then browning in a mixture of sunflower oil and butter until crisp.

Potato, Funghi Porcini and Truffle Ravioli Stuffing

For this recipe you need to have made the Cep and Truffle Relish (on page 77). From then on you simply boil 1 kg of autumn potatoes in their skins (i.e. not new). Désirée or other reds are particularly good. Drain thoroughly and peel while warm, transferring them to a bowl. Mash coarsely with a little olive oil and seasoning, then add a little chopped parsley and as much of the relish as you think is financially wise.

This to me is the star stuffing, but I find it impossible to give an exact recipe. Much Italian cooking is like that, it is a hand-me-down tradition and relies on observation and demonstration rather than slavishly following a recipe. However, if you have made the relish, then you can experiment with this one. Note well the instruction to drain the potatoes thoroughly; if you leave any residual cooking water, the stuffing will be sloppy and useless.

PASTA FAGIOLI | PASTA AND PULSES

These hearty dishes are found throughout Italy in numerous mutations. Basically they all have two things in common: pulses, be they cannellini, borlotti, fave or chick peas, and pasta cooked with them. To further confuse matters, there is a whole tribe of related dishes involving lentils and potatoes. Dietetically speaking, the combination of starch, protein and fibre in these dishes is wonderful.

Here I give a general all-purpose Pasta Fagioli using tinned beans, a general recipe for cooking pulses, a recipe for Pasta e Ceci (chickpeas, and Signor Belcapo's favourite), Pasta e Lenticche (lentils), and a curious but highly delicious Ligurian speciality, Pasta e Patate.

Pasta e Ceci
Chickpea Pasta

This presses the nostalgia button for most Italians, but is relatively unknown abroad. It's spicy, oily, mealy and cheesy (sounds disgusting), and is Signor Belcapo's favourite.

6 people
300 g ditali pasta
2 onions, 2 carrots, 1 celery stick, all
    peeled and cut into 3 mm dice
    for soffritto
4 garlic cloves, peeled and very
    finely chopped or minced
6 small dried chillies, very finely
    chopped or minced
100 g pancetta, cut into very
    small lardons
good olive oil

To cook the chickpeas, soak them in cold water overnight. They will double in size. Rinse extremely well and cover with water in a large pan. Bring to the boil over a high heat, turn down and skim off the very copious scum. Add the chickpea cooking ingredients and simmer for 1 1/2 hours, skimming occasionally. Taste for doneness, then allow to cool.

To bring the pasta e ceci together, put the soffritto, the garlic, chilli and pancetta with a little olive oil in a trustworthy casserole and sweat over a medium heat until lightly coloured and the pancetta has gone translucent, about 10–12 minutes. Add the tomato,

200 g tinned tomato pieces with
liquid (1 small tin)
1 big sprig rosemary, 1 bay leaf, a few
parsley stalks, 1 sprig thyme, tied
into a bouquet garni
Parmesan, freshly grated
Infused Oil (see page 187) or good
olive oil

For the chickpeas:

500 g chickpeas
1 large red chilli pepper
4 garlic cloves
2 bay leaves
1 sprig rosemary
2 sprigs parsley

bouquet garni and chickpeas, bring to a simmer then add enough water to cover the chickpeas by 3 cm. Bring back to a simmer and skim. Cook until the pancetta is tender, about 40 minutes.

When everything is ready, turn up the heat and add the pasta. Stir, return to the boil and cook, stirring often, for 5 minutes. Remove from the heat, cover and set aside for 10 minutes.

Grate the Parmesan. 100 g should be enough, but have more ready for the table.

Open the casserole and stir, adding the Parmesan and a good slug of infused oil or olive oil. Check the seasoning, particularly salt. The liquid should be nearly all absorbed by the pasta, leaving you with sauce-coated chickpeas and pasta. The pasta will have finished off cooking in the resting time. This is a fundamental Italian technique.

Little **Tip**

- Do not salt the chickpeas until they are tender, although paradoxically you can cook them with a ham hock which doesn't interfere with their tenderness. You can use tinned chickpeas if you insist, but please rinse them very thoroughly. The liquid gunk in the tin does not taste nice.

Reserve the leftover rosemary-cooked chickpeas in their liquor in an airtight plastic box in the fridge. Make into houmus or use for Cod and Chickpeas (see page 150). Brought to the boil every other day you should be able to keep them for over a week.

Pasta e Fagioli
Bean Pasta

Soup dish or pasta dish? To non-Italian eyes, a soup, to Italians a pasta dish, and not just any pasta dish – a national obsession. The Italians seem to regard them as vital to life as they know it – 'La vita fagioli'! Every region of Italy has a major variation; every former city state a slight modification; every village and every home their own version.

6 people
500 g ditali (not ditalini, these are
    too small)
500 g tinned fagioli, cannellini or
    borlotti beans, drained and
    rinsed thoroughly
good olive oil
1 carrot, 1 celery stick, 1 large onion,
    all peeled and cut into a fine
    soffritto
125 g pancetta, diced (optional)
1/2 large red chilli pepper, seeded
    and minced (or 4 small dried
    ones, reconstituted in a little
    water and chopped)
2 garlic cloves, peeled and minced
1 big sprig rosemary (reserve a few
    needles), 2 bay leaves, 1 sprig
    parsley, 1 sprig thyme, tied into a
    bouquet garni
1 x 500 g packet tomato passata
salt and pepper
Parmesan, freshly grated

Heat 4 tbsp oil in a heavy-bottomed casserole. Add the soffritto of diced vegetables and pancetta, if using, and sweat for 10 minutes over a medium heat. They may take on a little colour. Add the chilli, garlic and bouquet garni, and sweat for a further 5 minutes. Add the tomato passata, bring to a boil, stir thoroughly, then add 500 ml water and simmer until the vegetables are very tender. Add the beans and simmer for 10 minutes more.

While this is cooking, blanch the pasta: that is, put a 5 litre pan of water on to boil, salt it and boil the ditali for 4 minutes. Drain, refresh by plunging into cold water, then drain thoroughly and tip into a bowl. Lightly dress with olive oil to prevent it sticking together – you may add the reserved rosemary needles to this pasta for an interesting aromatic seasoning.

Remove the vegetable pan from the cooker, and discard the bouquet garni. Purée half the mixture and return to the remainder in the pan. At this point everything is ready, and can be held until you need it.

To serve, mix the pasta and beans together to make the soup. Heat gently until very hot and the pasta is al dente. Be careful as the dish will stick easily, scorch and spoil; keep gently stirring. Serve in soup plates with Parmesan, and some good oil added separately.

Little **Tip**

■ If this or any other dish is showing signs of sticking and burning, do not under any circumstances try to stir or scrape the offending part into the rest. Lift the pan from the cooker and quickly pour its contents into another bowl or pan. The spoilt part will remain in the pan and will hopefully not have marred the rest with the unremovable taste of charred food.

Pasta e Lenticche
Pasta and Lentils

This member of the pasta fagioli family is essentially Roman in character, and is rather more enterprisingly spiced than most Italian dishes. Northern Italians refer to Romans as Arabs and not politely, seeing themselves as essentially North European, and the Romans as belonging to the sensuous exotic south, to the Mediterranean. The Romans should be proud of the Arab connection shown so clearly in this dish.

6 people
150 g green or blue lentils
400 g spaghetti
4 tbsp good olive oil
1 tsp each of ground cumin and
    coriander
1 large red chilli, finely diced
1/4 tsp turmeric
1 celery stick, 1 large carrot and 1
    onion, peeled and finely diced to
    a soffritto
4 garlic cloves, peeled and chopped
2 bay leaves
1 tbsp grated fresh root ginger
    (optional)
Parmesan, freshly grated
Infused Oil (see page 187)

Soak the lentils for 1 hour in cold water to cover, then rinse.

Put 4 tbsp olive oil in a large pan and heat over a medium heat. Add the cumin, coriander, chilli and turmeric and sweat for 2 minutes. Add the soffritto and garlic and sweat for a further 5 minutes. Add the lentils, stir to coat thoroughly with oil, then cover with three times their volume of water. Bring to a simmer, add the bay leaves and ginger (if using), and cook until the lentils are tender. This will take approximately 45 minutes. The lentils can be held at this point, or drained and served as a vegetable. Remove the bay leaves.

Break the dry spaghetti into 2 cm lengths. Bring the lentil mix back to the boil. It should be approximately half liquid, but if it is a little dry, add some water. Add the spaghetti, return to a boil, and cook for 2 minutes, stirring occasionally. Switch off the heat, cover and leave for 10 minutes. As with the previous recipe, the pasta will continue cooking during the resting period, and will absorb a great deal of the liquid.

Serve with the Parmesan and infused oil.

Pasta e Patate
Pasta and Potatoes

This dish is from Liguria and Piedmont. I am assured this combination of carbohydrate on carbohydrate is, as I write, the latest thing dietetically. Scepticism remains, but this dish is certainly delicious, with a very home-cooked taste. All Italian males above the age of fourteen claim to be great cooks: the reality is different as most of them can't even make coffee, Mamma does it for them. They can talk about a great dish but would be lost if required to cook it. Fausto, one of the assistants at La Cacciata in 1995, rarely spoke at all before noon, and was hardly loquacious after that, so he completely shocked me one day by quietly producing this perfect dish. Fausto's Pasta e Patate.

6 people

300 g ditali (penne or macaroni)
500 g potatoes, peeled and cut
   into 5 mm dice
1.5 litres Chicken Broth (see
   page 186)
1 bunch parsley, leaves picked and
   finely chopped (keep the stems
   for the stock)
4 tbsp good olive oil, plus very
   good oil for the table
1 onion, peeled and very finely
   chopped
2 garlic cloves, peeled and finely
   minced
salt and coarsely ground black
   pepper
75 g Parmesan, freshly grated

Little **Tip**

■ Clingfilm and freeze all the
Parmesan rinds you can. A couple of
pieces dropped into a dish like this
or Pasta e Ceci (see page 84) add a
lot of flavour but must be fished out
before serving.

Heat the broth to boiling, add the parsley stalks, then simmer for a few minutes. In a trustworthy 4 litre pan or casserole heat the good oil over a medium heat and add the onions and garlic. Soften for a few moments, then add the potatoes and parsley. Stir and soften for a few minutes, still over a medium flame. The potatoes starting to stick will announce the end of this stage. Season with a little salt but rather more coarsely ground black pepper, then sieve all the broth in. Turn up the heat until boiling and then turn down to medium. Simmer until the potatoes are nearly tender then add the pasta. Return to a simmer, then stir and cook for 5 minutes. Stir again, cover and allow to sit off the heat for 5 minutes.

Remove the lid and stir gently again, adding the Parmesan. You stir gently because the potatoes should not break up completely. By now most of the liquid should have been absorbed by the pasta and everything is ready to eat, you merely need to adjust the seasoning. If still rather liquid but the pasta is al dente, serve anyway, telling your guests that it's always served like that in Genoa. Extra Parmesan and very good olive oil should be offered at the table.

GNOCCHI | DUMPLINGS

Gnocchi, literally 'dumplings', are found all over Italy, and confusingly fall into four main categories: light, airy dumplings made with ricotta cheese and spinach; occasionally light but sometimes heavy potato dumplings (not included here because of abject failures on my part to cook them even moderately edibly – I will try again); substantial semolina dumplings (very much a Roman speciality); and finally, various very heavy forms of pasta, usually resembling the larval stage of insects, which arc invariably boiled for a long time and then baked with sauces – I find them distinctly unappealing.

Gnocchi make a nice elegant starter for a dinner party, perhaps baked in individual dishes, or a light lunch, if served with a salad.

Malafatta/Strangolapreti/Gnocchi con Bietole
Ricotta and Spinach Dumplings

Three titles for the same dish from Emilia Romagna (northern Italy). 'Malafatta' means 'badly made', and refers to their inevitable home-made appearance. 'Strangolapreti' is my favourite, and means 'priest strangler', apocryphally referring to a greedy prelate's demise. 'Gnocchi con Bietole' is misleading in that these light dumplings bear little resemblance to all the other rather heavy gnocchi of Italy.

Ideally bietole or Swiss chard should be used for this dish but fresh spinach makes an acceptable substitute. (Incidentally, very well drained and squeezed frozen leaf spinach will do.)

The quality of the ricotta is important as, obviously, is that of the Parmesan. Try and seek out a better quality ricotta from your delicatessen or cheese shop, but don't worry if you have to use supermarket brands. This recipe contains virtually no flour in the mix, which I think improves on the Italian originals, but does make the dumplings harder to form. Under no circumstances use a food processor for the chopping of the spinach or the ricotta. The dumplings will be heavy if you do.

4–6 people
600 g spinach (or Swiss chard greens)
200 g ricotta cheese
salt and pepper
100 g Parmesan, freshly grated
plain flour
2 eggs
freshly grated nutmeg
200 g butter
12 sage leaves

To prepare and form the gnocchi

Cook the spinach by dipping it in salted boiling water for 1 minute, then draining and refreshing it in cold water. Drain again then, using your hands, squeeze as dry as possible; copious quantities of water will come out. Now squeeze again and even more will exude. When you are satisfied that it is as dry as you can get it (your arms will be aching but it does wonders for the pectoral muscles), re-fluff it up by breaking up the compacted balls. You will need to have 200 g – if you find yourself with a little less, adjust the other ingredients accordingly.

Coarsely chop the spinach and put in a large mixing bowl. Break up and add the ricotta, Parmesan, 150 g of the flour and the eggs. Mix partially then season with freshly grated nutmeg, salt and pepper. Now mix thoroughly and refrigerate for an hour.

To form the gnocchi, place 200 g flour on a tray and season it well. Lightly dust another tray with more flour, and flour your hands. Take a gobstopper sized piece of the mixture and roll in your floured hands until a smooth ball is formed, then roll in the seasoned flour until coated and transfer to the lightly floured tray. Re-flour your hands and repeat. You will have appallingly messy hands after a while. Refrigerate the formed gnocchi until needed. Clear what seems to be the entire kitchen as this is a messy job.

To cook and serve the gnocchi

Preheat the oven to 110°C/225°F/Gas 1/4. Heat an attractive ovenproof dish (which is big enough to hold the gnocchi in a single layer) in the low oven. Put a wide shallow pan of water on to boil and add salt.

Put the butter to melt with the sage leaves in a small saucepan and infuse. Do not burn, just melt it and keep warm. Carefully tip the formed gnocchi into the boiling water and return to a simmer. As soon as bubbles reappear, turn down the heat to maintain a simmer. The gnocchi take 10 minutes or so to cook and they float when done. Of course if you didn't use a wide pan and foolishly opted for a deep, narrow saucepan, many of the dumplings will be held under by their colleagues on top. They will not be able to demonstrate their buoyant personalities and will become waterlogged.

Remove the heated dish from the oven and turn the oven up to 180°C/350°/Gas 4. When the gnocchi are cooked drain with a spider very carefully (they are fragile) and place in a single layer in the heated dish. A little water will cling to them. Pour over the melted butter and sage and return to the oven for 10 minutes. Serve in the dish at the table, and pass more Parmesan if you like the idea.

Little **Tip**

■ For cooking large quantities of gnocchi or ravioli, a deep roasting dish with about 5 cm water in it is ideal; you may need to put it over two burners. The reason for this is that you have a high surface area of water in relation to the depth, and all the individual gnocchi can be watched closely as they cook without too much stirring, which damages them.

Gnocchi alla Romana
Baked Semolina Gnocchi

This is unavoidably a two-day process. Fortunately, it only involves half an hour's work on day one, and less on day two. It is a winter antipasto, heavy, rich and hideously fattening, but quite addictive.

6 people
Day One
1 litre milk
400 g coarse semola dura (the semolina *must* be Italian)
200 g Parmesan, freshly grated
6 egg yolks
50 g butter

Day Two
60 g butter
50 g Parmesan, freshly grated

Day One
Heat the milk in a trustworthy pan until warm then add the semolina. Pour it in slowly, steadily stirring all the time (it's best for two people, if possible, to do this – one to pour, one to stir). Continue to stir over a medium heat for 15–20 minutes until the semolina forms a mass coming away from the side of the pan.

Allow this mixture to cool a little, then add the Parmesan, egg yolks and butter. Mix very well. Lightly oil a Swiss roll tin or roasting dish and pour the mixture into it. It should not be deeper than 2 cm. Allow to cool completely, then clingfilm and refrigerate overnight.

Day Two
An hour before serving, preheat the oven to 200°C/400°F/Gas 6. You will need a large shallow ovenproof dish (an oval Le Creuset would be ideal), and a 4 cm circular (cookie) cutter.

Butter the ovenproof dish. Cut the semolina into 4 cm circles and arrange them overlapping like roof tiles around the circumference of the dish. Start another oval within this and continue until you have either filled the dish or run out of semolina to cut. If you have run out before the dish is full, use the off cuts from between the circles to fill the gaps. The gnocchi discs should overlap so much they are standing nearly vertically. Dot the completed dish with butter and scatter the Parmesan over. Bake until very hot and golden brown on all the raised edges, 15–20 minutes approximately.

Serve directly from the dish, still very hot. Serve your guests yourself, otherwise they will inevitably burn themselves on the hot dish.

CRESPELLE | PANCAKES

Savoury pancakes in Italy form an alternative to pasta. They can be substituted for lasagne, but more normally are used as cannelloni. In the north the stuffing tends to involve spinach, Parmesan, various other cheeses and butter; in the south minced pork or veal would figure strongly.

Anelli di Ricotta e Spinaci
Spinach and Ricotta Pancakes

Another dish from Emilia Romagna, featuring a stuffing of spinach, ricotta and Parmesan, substituting pasta with pancakes. This dish is also found in Florence, under the title of Crespelle alla Fiorentina (I thought a display of my arcane intimacy with regional Italian cooking and dialects was in order). Frozen leaf spinach drained very well is good for this dish. You will also need a non-stick Swiss roll tray.

4–6 people
For the pancakes:
150 g plain flour
4 eggs
400 ml water
40 g butter, melted
a little salt

For the stuffing:
150 g ricotta cheese
150 g mascarpone cheese
150 g Parmesan, grated
150 g cooked spinach or Swiss
    chard, finely chopped
salt and pepper
freshly grated nutmeg

To serve:
40 g butter
40 g Parmesan, freshly grated

Little Tip

■ These stuffed pancakes can also be reheated as cannelloni, left whole and baked in a tray with Béchamel Sauce (see page 189) and a Rich Tomato Sauce (see page 189).

For the stuffing, combine the cheeses in a food processor and purée, then mix with the spinach in a bowl, seasoning with salt, pepper and a little nutmeg. Refrigerate while you make the pancakes.

Combine the flour and eggs in a mixer then add the water and half the melted butter. Season and set aside. Preheat the oven to its maximum and put your Swiss roll tin into it to heat. Remove and butter lightly, then put a small ladle of the pancake batter in this and tilt to coat evenly. Return to the oven for 3 minutes or until set. Allow to cool a little and then repeat until you have one rectangular pancake per person.

To assemble, divide the stuffing into as many portions as you have pancakes. Lay one pancake with a long edge nearest you. Place a portion of the stuffing formed into a rough cylinder 1 cm in from this leading edge and stopping 1 cm from each end. Roll up the pancake to form a neat cylinder and fold in the ends. Refrigerate until you have made them all. These can be assembled up to a day ahead.

To cook and serve, preheat the oven to 180°C/350°F/Gas 4. Melt the butter, and use a little to butter a large gratin dish. Cut the pancake rolls into 2 cm deep cylinders and arrange these packed tightly in the gratin dish. Pour the remaining melted butter on top, and pour a few drops of water into the base of the dish to help prevent sticking and burning. Dust lightly with grated Parmesan, and bake, loosely covered, for 15 minutes or until a tested centrally placed cylinder is hot in the middle.

93

4

Pizze, Pane e Polenta

Pizzas, Bread and Polenta The farmhouse and all the cottages at La Cacciata have outside wood-burning bread ovens. Several are derelict, but the one behind the farmhouse is used regularly and consists of a stone domed chamber with a flagstoned floor. There is no chimney, and smoke escapes out of the small door and is drawn up a flue positioned above. Filled with burning vine and olive trimmings, this oven can reach inferno-like temperatures (500°C). When the fire dies down a little, the oven retains much of its temperature; the ashes and embers are swept to the side of the oven, leaving a clear channel of glowing flagstone on which to cook pizze.

Focaccia and pizza are amongst the most primitive of breads, indeed the word focaccia is derived from the Roman 'panis focacius' or hearth bread, a simple leavened dough baked in the ashes of a fire. I have a simple recipe for a basic dough which will make pizza, focaccia, calzone and a delicious olive-oil bread. This dough calls for a food mixer with a dough hook. A food processor can be used, but is rather a brutal process, cutting and mashing the dough rather than stretching and kneading it. Working bread dough by hand is a hard physical process, good for bust (or pectoral) development and in a manual sort of way satisfying; it also produces by far the best results.

Pizze are prepared at La Cacciata by a Neapolitan gentleman whose name is Francesco but answers to his surname Ruocco. He looks like a slightly chubby angelic version of Sylvester Stallone and cooks like a dream. He makes his dough by hand, kneading ferociously with his Popeye-sized forearms bulging. When all the donkey work is done he lets the guests have a go shaping the individual dough balls, discreetly reshaping anything he considers too amateurish.

The pizza evening at the school is a genteel version of the Sangria and Wet T-shirt evenings of a Club 18 to 30 holiday. The food is cooked and consumed by hand outside, lots and lots of wine is drunk, and everyone has a go at making a pizza and, even more difficult, getting it on to the wooden paddle and into the oven. The only people who haven't enjoyed this evening have been a couple of rather arch, over-sophisticated hackettes from London who chose their free holiday perk as a chance to be sneery. No more not-so fragrant hackettes in the future.

A great deal of nonsense is talked about Italian bread – how wonderful and rustic it is. The reality is somewhat different. Bread is sold by weight in Italy, rarely includes any salt because salt is taxed (sold at tobacconists, for some arcane reason), and it is in the bakers' interests to get the heaviest loaf he can manage. This is not conducive to quality bread. My mother described the local bread at La Cacciata as instant duck food. It does, however, make excellent toast, crostini and bruschetta.

This situation is improving as more and more Italians travel abroad and become dissatisfied with what up to then seemed a perfectly satisfactory product. The Marchesa Franca Spinola, the chairperson of the Grosseto Chamber of Commerce (Grosseto is the capital of southern Tuscany), recently refused to renew all the bakers' annual licences until they produced a loaf to her liking. She is an extraordinary person, holding a position of authority rarely accorded to Italian women. Her family make wonderful wines and on her own estate, La Parrina, she has developed quite outstanding goat's cheeses, organic fruit and vegetables, olive oil, several wines, honeys and yoghurts which she retails in her three very chi-chi boutiques in Rome.

Bread Dough

This is an all-purpose dough, developed jointly between La Cacciata and Richard Whittington's Wandsworth kitchen.

500 ml warm water
1/2 sachet dried yeast
1 tsp caster sugar
900 g bread flour, plus extra for
    dusting
1 tbsp good olive oil
2 tsp sea salt

In a large bowl, combine the water, yeast and the sugar. (Omit the salt at this point, although salt doesn't automatically kill dried yeast.) Add half the flour, and stir with your fingertips until you have a very sloppy paste indeed. Gradually add the rest of the flour, plus the oil and salt, working with your fingers until you have a merely moist ball of dough. Dust the bowl of your food mixer with flour, and transfer the dough ball to it. With the dough hook, knead on a low speed for about 10 minutes.

You will now need a large floured tray. Flour your hands liberally and detach a piece of dough, the size roughly of a tangerine (halfway between a golf ball and tennis ball). Roll into a perfect sphere in your hands and place neatly on the floured tray. Repeat until all the dough is used up. Flour lightly and cover with a very slightly damp teatowel. Place in a warm room (21°C/70°F) for 2 hours to rise. The bread is now ready to make pizze or focaccia.

Little **Tip**

■ You may wish to reserve some of the dough for other uses, in which case detach half, and allow to rise for 2 hours in a floured bowl covered with a teatowel. Punch down and keep in the fridge in a floured zip-lock bag. It has been known to remain alive and feisty for up to 3 days like this. When you wish to use it, remove from the fridge 2 hours in advance of cooking. The raising of the temperature will re-awaken the yeast.

■ Ciabatta is an over-proved bread in that it has been allowed to rise for too long in conventional terms, developing the characteristic large holes which you pay for. Simply make the bread dough, adding an extra tbsp of olive oil, but allow to rise for 4 hours. Punch down, shape into slipper-like shapes, lie on a floured baking sheet, cover again and allow to rise for a further 2 hours or even overnight in the fridge. Bake in a medium oven (180°C/350°F/Gas 4) until risen and crusty. Precise timing is difficult here, practice makes perfect. Leftover ciabatta makes excellent crostini, breadcrumbs or bruschetta.

Pizzetta Bianca
White Pizza

A thin focaccia topped with rosemary, garlic and chilli, moistened with olive oil, and finished with crisp sea salt. After the guests have had the wonders of Ruocco's pizza, they complain that they could never duplicate the oven (except for one architect who went home and built himself one), and therefore need not even try. To counter this I make this simple dish and cook it in a domestic oven. The results speak for themselves.

Up to 10 people
1 recipe Bread Dough (see
    page 97), divided into tangerine-
    sized balls
good olive oil
1 small dried chilli, minced
1 garlic clove, peeled and minced
1 sprig rosemary
bread flour
Maldon sea salt

■ One of the most frequently asked
questions at La Cacciata is 'Can I
do this in an Aga?' (does this reflect
the demographic distribution of the
guests?). The answer with pizze
has to be a resounding yes. Make
sure your Aga is as hot as it can
possibly go. Assemble the pizzetta
on its flan base and slide directly on
to the cast-iron base of the hot
roasting oven – preferably near the
front as retrieving it may be difficult.

You will need two baking sheets, a rolling pin, and the base of a loose-bottomed flan ring, the bigger the better.

Preheat the oven to its maximum well in advance, as it must be as hot as you can get it. Put 6 tbsp olive oil in a small pan and set over a very low heat, then add the chilli and garlic. Infuse and warm for 10 minutes then remove from the heat and add the stripped rosemary needles.

Put the baking sheets in your very hot oven. Cover your work surface liberally with flour and press one ball of dough on it with the heel of your hand until it forms a 1 cm thick disc. Flour the rolling pin and roll out into a 20 cm oval by only rolling in one direction. Turn this oval through 90 degrees and roll in one direction away from you. You will now have a rough circle. Flour your hands and lift the dough circle and sweep more flour under it, then with your hands press the dough into a very thin and regular circle, trying to leave the edges a little thicker. Flour the flan ring base and, holding at a 20 degree angle, quickly insert it under the dough.

Dribble the pizzetta lightly with some of the flavoured oil, making sure some garlic, rosemary and chilli goes with it. Do not swamp and do not allow the oil to run over the edge of the pizzetta as this will prevent rising. Slide this pizzetta off the flan base on to one of the baking sheets in the oven and cook for 8–10 minutes until brown, slightly risen and bubbly. Immediately you put it in the oven start another one, it will be needed! Serve hot sprinkled with sea salt, and drink a coarse red wine with it. Don't burn yourself in your greed.

Previous page
Clockwise from left: Pizzetta Bianca, Pizza con Patate e Rucola,
Variation on Pizzetta Bianca.

Little Tips and Variations

■ There are innumerable toppings you can put on this type of bread but remember the *bread* is the point, any flavourings should only be sparsely scattered. Here are a few suggestions: sliced raw red onions, sage, salt and olive oil; diced black olives and chilli with oil; diced sun-dried tomatoes, coarse black pepper, salt and oil; anchovies, diced with sliced onion.

■ Never oil the baking sheet or flan base. Flour in copious quantities is the lubricant, and its slightly charred flavour when cooked is an important element of the dish's taste. For this dish the dough must be rolled as thin as humanly possible, and the laying on of hands as described above is the best method. It's your pizza and your kitchen.

The cooking time given in these recipes is not absolute, it all depends on how hot your oven will go. A shorter time is unlikely, but up to 5 minutes more may be necessary. A pizza base ideally should be crisp on the rim and on the base, but must be tender and pliant as well. This is achieved by a very high cooking temperature.

Pizza Margarita
Tomato Pizza

The classic pizza – nothing else comes near in terms of simplicity, balance and general all-round political correctness.

Up to 8 people
1 recipe Bread Dough (see page 97), divided into tangerine-sized balls
1 x 500 g tin best-quality tomato pieces
salt and pepper
good olive oil
a handful of basil leaves, shredded
1 buffalo mozzarella, very finely diced

Preheat the oven to its maximum, and put the baking sheets in the oven as for the previous recipe.

Tip the tomato pieces into a bowl, and season generously. Mix in a good slug of olive oil and add the shredded basil leaves. This is the tomato sauce base for all pizze involving tomato, with a distinct lack of cooking.

Roll out a circle of dough as for the previous recipe.

Smear the pizza base with about 2 tbsp of the sauce, using the back of the spoon to spread it. Leave a 2 cm band of clear dough all the way round. Scatter lightly with mozzarella dice. Season the pizza and sprinkle with olive oil (this oil on top is important, it speeds up the cooking of the pizza top while the by now very hot baking sheet is coping with the bottom). Bake for 8–10 minutes until the rim has risen and browned and the topping is bubbling viciously.

Immediately start making another one. Never make pizza wait, it should be eaten as soon as possible.

Pizza con Patate e Rucola
Pizza with Potato and Rocket

Potato pizza has been an obsession of mine since 1978 when I first tasted it in Rome near Termini station. It sounds heavy, and my first attempts were just that, but they steadily improved over the years. Then along came Ruocco and this sensational dish.

Up to 8 people
1 recipe Bread Dough (see page 97)
a handful Salad of Rocket per
    pizza (see page 38)
2 large potatoes, peeled
salt and pepper
1 buffalo mozzarella, diced
1 sprig rosemary
good olive oil

Preheat the oven to its maximum with the baking trays inside.

Using a mandolin or food processor slicer blade, cut the potatoes into as thin slices as possible then put into a bowl of cold water to de-starch.

Roll out two pizza bases as in the previous recipes. Take a small handful of sliced potatoes and wring out dry, then spread around the bases, leaving a clear rim. Season well, then dot with mozzarella dice, scatter with a few rosemary needles, and drizzle with a little oil. Bake for 10 minutes until the potatoes are browning. Serve a little rocket salad in a mound on top of the hot pizza. Share these ones and start baking two more, they will be needed.

Crostini alla Toscana

What are crostini? Croûtons, pure and simple, with toppings. A big selection can be visually magnificent. This is *the* classic crostini dish.

4 people
4 large slices Tuscan-style bread
120 g chicken livers (plus some
    hearts if available), trimmed well
good olive oil
1/2 white onion, peeled and very
    finely diced
2 tbsp Vin Santo (or other sweet
    fortified wine)
1/2 tsp balsamic vinegar
salt and pepper
4 ripe tomatoes, peeled (optional)
4 basil leaves

To prepare the livers, heat a little olive oil in a medium frying pan over a medium heat. Add the onion and sweat for 2–3 minutes until translucent. Add the livers and continue to cook for 15–20 minutes, stirring occasionally. Add the Vin Santo and vinegar and some salt and pepper, then give a brief boil over a high heat. Set aside to cool. Mash with a fork, add a little more oil, transfer to a bowl and refrigerate until needed.

To prepare the tomatoes, peel them if you wish, and cut into 5 mm circular slices. Season, dress with a little oil, and set aside in a bowl.

To prepare the crostini, preheat the grill. Cut each slice of bread into four pieces and arrange on a baking sheet. Drizzle with oil, then grill until brown. Spread with either the liver or the tomatoes.

Crostini con Crema di Fagioli Cannellini
Crostini with Puréed Haricot Beans

This dish is almost an Italian houmus. We give here the basic recipe for cooking fagioli: it applies, with slightly varied cooking times, for borlotti and fave. The beans make enough to feed ten people; store the remainder in the fridge and use for Tonno e Fagioli, Pasta Fagioli and various minestrones (see pages 49, 84 and 52).

4–6 people
4–6 large slices Tuscan-style bread
good olive oil
a handful of parsley
juice of 1 lemon

For the puréed beans:
500 g dried cannellini beans, soaked
    overnight
1 red chilli
4 garlic cloves, in their skins
2 bay leaves
1 sprig rosemary
parsley stalks

Little **Tip**

- The remaining beans should be returned to the cooking liquor and stored covered in the fridge.

Rinse the beans very thoroughly. Put in a large pan and cover to twice their depth with cold water (the volume of the soaked beans and the water should be the same: use the soaking bowl to measure). Bring the beans to a boil, turn the heat down, and skim thoroughly. Add the other ingredients and continue to simmer at a low heat until tender. The cooking time will vary according to the relative dryness of the beans, anything from 40 minutes to 2 hours.

Allow the beans to cool in their liquor. Drain, keeping the cooking water.

Prepare the crostini as above, drizzling with oil and grilling.

Take 250 g of cooked beans, preferably still warm (but you may reheat) and 4 tbsp of their cooking liquor, the garlic cloves from the recipe (peeled) and half the chilli. Place in a food processor and whizz. Add and blend in the parsley, the lemon juice and, finally, about 100 ml good olive oil. Spread on the grilled crostini and serve.

Bruschetta
Garlic Toast

Quite simply a slice of robust white bread grilled, then rubbed with a clove of garlic (cut it in half, do not peel), sprinkled with salt and drizzled with good, very fresh olive oil. It is best done on a barbecue, but satisfactory results can be obtained with an electric toaster.

Bruschetta in Umbria is rarely served with anything on it – usually a local quite salty ham is offered on a separate plate – but a wonderful variation is to coarsely dice some very ripe tomatoes, season and add a little oil. (No onion, no basil.) Leave this in a bowl to go slightly soupy. Make bruschetta and heap with the tomato mix. Eat with a knife and fork immediately, it's too soggy to eat by hand.

POLENTA

Polenta is cornmeal porridge and to first tastes is about as attractive as it sounds (second and third tastes too). It has virtually no nutritive value, in fact people from poor polenta-eating areas, mainly in the Alps, suffered from various deficiency diseases due to their dependence on the stuff. Not only this, but it requires 45 minutes' standing and stirring to cook – no wonder the diehards of the food world love it; it's tedious to prepare and tastes like grainy wallpaper paste.

However, bowing to peer pressure, there are ways of making the stuff more than edible. Firstly, the Italians make it with virtually no additions, a little butter and a little cheese perhaps, but they talk about the purity of taste and texture. These are precisely the qualities I strive to hide, so use plenty of butter and lots of grated Parmesan, please. Secondly, the purists also insist that only raw polenta will do; bullshit, buy the instant stuff and follow the packet instructions. Thirdly, the only good polenta is set polenta; a flaccid mound of wet polenta on your plate is something to avoid. Let your polenta set like concrete, then slice and grill, the charring from this process hiding its more unpleasant attributes.

Polenta alla Griglia
Grilled Polenta

This is my basic recipe for cooking polenta. If you insist on cooking raw polenta, merely increase the cooking time from 5 minutes to 45, and stand there and stir. Secondly, if you further insist on serving the polenta wet, i.e. as a porridge, halt at the appropriate part in the recipe.

Incidentally, wet polenta is almost impossible to reheat, so time it to coincide with your main course being ready. I am being rather hard on wet polenta. It provides an interesting sop to various Italian meat dishes which have plenty of gravy. However, I personally prefer mashed potato in this role.

6 people
250 g instant polenta (Star is a
    good brand)
120 g butter
750 ml water
salt and pepper
100 g Parmesan, freshly grated (or
    half Parmesan, half Gruyère)
100 ml double cream or crème
    fraîche (optional)

You will need a wide, deep baking tray, buttered (use about 20 g). Bring the water to the boil, season it, then pour in the polenta in a steady stream, stirring vigorously with the spoon in your other hand. Turn the heat to medium and cook, stirring, until it boils. Now turn the heat to low, and simmer for 5 minutes. Be careful when you stir, as the stuff tends to imitate volcanic mud on boiling, and large bubbles surface and explode messily. Take from the heat and stir in the remaining butter, then stir in the grated cheese. Adjust the seasoning and pour into the buttered tray; it should be a minimum of 2 cm deep. Bang the tray gently on the table to level the glop, and allow to cool. Refrigerate.

Cut into 1 cm slices and grill on the barbecue or in a ridged grill pan until nicely brown. It will shrink a little. Don't attempt to move it once it's on the grill but leave for a minimum of 5 minutes before turning, this should help prevent sticking.

5

Risotti

QUESTIONS AND ANSWERS

How to cook a perfect risotto has become a holy grail. We, the late twentieth-century British, true to form, embraced the dish and immediately set about debasing it. Depressing recipes tell you that it is too much trouble to make in the correct manner and insist on putting it in the oven – sheer heresy. Basically, and with typical Italian elegance, the dish is the only delicious way of preparing the rather odd breeds of their native rice.

What is risotto and how do I cook it?

See the basic Risotto con Parmigiano recipe opposite. The whole process, not including heating the stock, should take 30 minutes. Sounds simple, and it is, so why should it be perceived as difficult? Because it is a rigorous and inviolate methodology you must not deviate from it, or you will at best have an ersatz risotto and at worst a vile glop.

How much rice do I use?

There are three methods of measuring. For us, 60 g per person; for an Italian housewife, 1 delicate handful per person; and for a more fastidious Italian chef, 1 espresso cup. They sometimes add 1 more handful or cup for the pot.

What is the best pan for risotto?

Any pan that distributes the heat evenly. I have very good results with Le Creuset type cast-iron casseroles. Rice has a tendency to stick and burn in the corner of pans between bottom and side so look for a pan with a nice round profile here. The pan chosen should be wide rather than deep and should have a lid. Any pan can be used to heat the stock.

Can I cook risotto in large quantities in the same way?

Yes, doubling or trebling risotto amounts does not affect the cooking time. At La Cacciata we frequently do it for 30 people, and it takes approximately 35 minutes. Remember you will need a suitably large pan and that the rice expands threefold during cooking.

Can I use any rice other than Italian?

No. Arborio is the easiest rice to find. Vialone and carnaroli are other Italian types and have their adherents. Venetians favour vialone but their Risotto Nero is considered best made with carnaroli. Do not attempt to use pudding, patna or Japanese rice, despite their similar appearance to Italian rice.

Do you use olive oil or butter for risotto?

Rice is grown in the Po Valley in northern Italy, where the principal cooking fat is butter. With the exception of certain seafood risotti (see page 113), butter is always used for this dish.

What degree of liquidity should a perfect risotto have?

A perfect risotto is not a mound of stodgy rice on a plate sitting like a glutinous mound, nor is it a soupy liquid mess lying flat in the plate. It should be just about moundable, fighting to hold its little peaks from collapsing back into the rest. It should have no free liquid as the final application of butter and cheese, coupled with 3 minutes' rest, will result in the broth coating the rice.

What do I serve risotto in at the table?

Take the risotto to the table in its cooking pan and serve in wide, shallow soup plates. In Milan you can observe risotto addicts gently pushing their ambrosia up the side of the plate, spreading it and cooling it. I find this a trifle absurd; the rice will not significantly overcook on the plate. However, it will be completely ruined if left to sit for too long. Like pasta and pizza, it waits for no one.

How do restaurants serve risotto?

In general they don't – they serve a bastardised version involving part cooking and reheating. There is no point in imitating chefs here. Restaurants that are very serious about risotto in Italy cook it to order, and quite wonderful it is too, especially when you have waited half an hour for it.

Risotto con Parmigiano

Risotto with Parmesan

This is the prototypical risotto. With the addition of saffron and bone marrow it becomes Risotto Milanese, a subject of near mystical status in Lombardy.

4 people

240 g arborio rice
1.2 litres Chicken Broth (see page 186
    or use 2 chicken stock cubes)
80 g butter
1/2 onion, peeled and finely chopped
    (ok to use a food processor)
75 g Parmesan, freshly grated
salt and pepper

Bring the stock to a simmer, next to where you will cook the risotto. Take a wide, heavy-bottomed pan or casserole, put half the butter in over a medium heat, and melt. Add the onion and sweat until it softens and becomes slightly translucent, about 5 minutes. Add the rice and stir with a wooden spoon until it is thoroughly coated in butter, about 2 minutes. Then take a soup ladle of hot stock and pour into the rice. Continue to cook and stir until this liquid addition is completely absorbed, about 3 minutes.

Repeat this procedure several times until the rice has swollen and is nearly tender. The rice should not be soft but neither should it be chalky. Taste and wait: if it is undercooked, it will leave a gritty, chalky residue in your mouth. Normally the rice is ready about 20 minutes after the first addition of stock. If it is taking much longer, the heat is too low or your rice has been hanging around in the store cupboard for too long.

Now the enrichment. Add the other half of the butter and half the Parmesan. Stir these in, season and cover. Leave to rest and swell a little more for 3 minutes. Serve immediately after this in soup plates, with more Parmesan offered separately.

Risotto con Funghi
Mushroom Risotto

Mushrooms – here dried funghi porcini and large flat cultivated ones – are sweated with onions and butter as a flavour basis for the rice. The stock is enriched with the dried funghi porcini soaking water, white wine, and the stems and peelings from the flats. A little of the dried funghi porcini go a long way to flavouring this wonderful dish. I first ate this at Adam Robinson's Brackenbury restaurant: trust Adam to get all that mushroom flavour into the dish for relatively little outlay – constructive cheating!

It is essential you make the stock but you can leave the chicken stock cubes out if those picky vegetarians are coming again. Other sorts of mushrooms, magic etc., can be substituted, girolles spring to mind.

4–6 people
300 g arborio rice
500 g large flat open cultivated
    mushrooms
60 g dried funghi porcini, soaked in
    1 litre warm water
75 g butter
1 onion, peeled and very finely diced
75 g Parmesan, freshly grated

For the mushroom stock
2 carrots, washed
2 celery sticks
2 onions
the stalks and peelings from the
    flat mushrooms
2 glasses white wine
4 chicken stock cubes (Knorr are
    the best)
1 bay leaf

- Don't worry if, as your risotto nears completion, the stock appears to be running low. Boil a kettle and add water to the risotto to extend. You will not be short of flavour.

Peel the mushrooms and de-stalk them, reserving the peelings and stalks for the stock. Slice the caps of the mushrooms finely.

To make the stock, do not peel the vegetables. Put them into the processor and chop. Place in a large pan with the mushroom stalks and peelings, wine and stock cubes, add the bay leaf and cover with 4 litres water. Boil vigorously for 1 hour. Sieve and discard the vegetables and return the liquid to the boil until it is reduced by half. Cool and refrigerate, if not using immediately.

To make the risotto, bring the reduced stock to a simmer. Melt half the butter over a medium heat and add the minced onion. Sauté or sweat for 5 minutes, but do not allow to burn. Add the sliced caps of the mushrooms and continue sweating until they collapse and render liquid.

At this point drain the funghi porcini with a slotted spoon or your hand. Do not disturb the remnants of the forest floor sitting sediment-like in the bowl, and do not throw the liquor away. Add the funghi porcini to the mushroom and onion mix, then stir and add the rice. Continue sweating together for a further 5 minutes. While this is happening, carefully sieve the funghi porcini soaking juices through a tea strainer and add to the stock.

Now you can proceed as for the other risotti by adding stock as needed, and only adding a further ladle when the previous lot is completely absorbed. When the rice is done add the remaining butter and the Parmesan, stir and cover. Leave to rest for 3 minutes and then serve immediately, with more Parmesan offered separately.

Risotto d'Asparagi
Asparagus Risotto

For me, one of the best of all risotti. You will need to make an asparagus stock, which is unavoidable, but it can be done in advance.

4–6 people
300 g arborio rice
500 g medium to large asparagus
    stalks, peeled and trimmed
    (reserve the ends and peelings
    for the stock)
125 g butter
1 large onion, peeled and very, very
    finely chopped
75 g Parmesan, freshly grated

For the asparagus stock:
2 carrots, peeled
2 celery sticks, stringed
2 onions, peeled
asparagus ends and peelings
1 bay leaf
salt and pepper

Pulse the stock vegetables together in a food processor until fine. Put with the bay leaf into a 6 litre pot and cover with water, at least 4 litres. Season and bring to the boil. Boil for 30 minutes, then sieve. Discard the vegetables and return the stock to the boil, reducing it to concentrate the flavour until you are left with about 2 litres. Cool and refrigerate if not using immediately.

To make the risotto, heat the stock to a simmer. Cut the asparagus stalks into 5 mm slanted slices. Take your chosen pan and add half the butter and the onion. Sweat over a medium heat for 5 minutes, then add the asparagus. Sweat for 5 minutes more, then add the rice. Sweat, stirring, until the rice sticks, then add 2 ladles of stock. Stirring, cook until the liquid is absorbed and the rice begins to stick. Repeat as for the previous recipes.

When the rice is nearly done turn off the heat and add the remaining butter and then the grated Parmesan. Season, stir, cover and leave for 3 minutes.

Risotto Nero
Cuttlefish Risotto with Ink

A frightening dish to prepare at home, the colour is so daunting. You will need a cooperative fishmonger who can find the cuttlefish and prepare them for you. I find that this dish is only worth preparing with cuttlefish, as the flavour of the ink is incomparable. Squid ink by contrast is bitter and disappointing, and the packaged inks are completely tasteless, a problem that restaurant chefs get around by using a good fish stock. This recipe uses a very dilute stock – i.e. water – and relies on a glass of dry white wine going in early on for flavour.

Ask your fishmonger to order the cuttlefish for you, and specify that they must be small (200 g each, maximum). Ask him to clean them for you and tell him you *must* have the sacs still intact. Chinese fishmongers often have cuttlefish, but you may have difficulty conveying your instructions to them, and even if you did they would think you mad. Black food is considered very bad joss in China.

6 people
300 g rice (ideally carnaroli, but
    arborio is fine)
500 g cuttlefish
1.2 litres hot water, infused with a
    bay leaf, parsley stalks, salt
    and pepper
1 glass dry white wine
1 onion, peeled and very finely diced
50 g butter
a few parsley leaves, coarsely
    chopped
salt and pepper

Bring the water to the boil with the flavourings, and simmer for 30 minutes to infuse. Open the wine and have a glass! Take the cuttlefish and cut into bite-sized chunks. Put the onion on to sweat in half the butter and cook until soft and translucent, then add the cuttlefish and sweat for about half an hour until nearly tender. It will render quite a lot of liquid. You do not need to pay much attention to the cuttlefish as they cook, but you do need to prepare the ink sacs.

Take a soup plate and with a small sharp knife cut 1 ink sac. Using the back of the blade, push the semi-solid ink out into the plate. You will need to hold the sac with the back of a teaspoon. Repeat with the other ink sacs and put the empty sacs into your infusing water; do not wash the knife or spoon, rinse them off in the water as well. Add a small amount of the wine to the soup plate and mix to a jet black liquid.

Add the rice to the cuttlefish and stir, then add the ink and rinse out the plate with the remaining wine. Add this to the cuttlefish and rice. Now add a ladle of the now grey and infused water (hereinafter described as the water) and stir, still over a medium heat, until absorbed. Repeat this step until the rice is cooked al dente. Add the remaining butter and the parsley leaves, stir, check the seasoning and cover. Leave to rest for 3 minutes, then serve immediately.

It is very important that the cuttlefish is nearly cooked before you add the rice. Small ones take less time, bigger ones may need more than half an hour's pre-cooking.

Risotto ai Frutti di Mare
Seafood Risotto

I first ate this splendid southern Italian rice dish in the courtyard of a handsome villa in Positano.

6 people
300 g arborio rice

1 kg mussels, bearded, scraped and checked for dead ones (open)

500 g Greenland shell-on prawns

500 g vongole veraci (palourde clams, optional)

500 g squid, cleaned and cut into bite-size pieces

4 tbsp good olive oil

1 onion, peeled and finely chopped

2 garlic cloves, peeled and minced

1 pinch saffron (12 stamens), infused in a little stock

1 large handful parsley leaves, chopped (keep the stalks for the stock)

For the stock:
1 bottle dry white wine

1 carrot, coarsely chopped

1 onion, peeled and coarsely chopped

2 celery sticks, coarsely chopped

2 tbsp tomato paste

1 bay leaf

To start the stock, put the mussels in a wide, lidded pan (they must not be stacked more than 2 shells deep). Add the whole bottle of wine, cover and bring to the boil over a high heat. Give them a shake and continue cooking fiercely until the mussels open. Pour the lot through a colander into a bowl and leave to drain and cool.

Next, peel and behead the prawns (reserve the tails in the fridge, try not to eat too many!). Put all the prawn peelings in a medium saucepan with the stock vegetables, tomato paste, bay leaf and the stalks from the parsley, add 1.5 litres of water and bring to a simmer over a medium flame. Skim.

When the mussels are cool, transfer to a tray still in their shells, moisten with a little of their liquor, then clingfilm and refrigerate. Sieve the winy mussel liquor into the stock and skim again. Simmer the stock for 1 hour, then sieve and discard all the debris. Return to the boil, skim and reduce a little. Check the seasoning but be careful; mussel liquor tends to be salty. (This stock is also an excellent basis for fish soups and sauces.)

To make the risotto, heat the olive oil in your risotto pan, add the finely diced onion and garlic, then sweat until soft and translucent. Add the rice and sweat, stirring, until coated with oil and glistening. Add a soup ladle of stock and continue cooking and stirring until the liquid is absorbed. Repeat this procedure several times until the rice is ready.

Add the squid after the rice has been cooking for 15 minutes. The vongole have to be opened, so as soon as you drop the squid into the rice put the clams to open in a wide, lightly oiled frying pan over a very high heat. Pick them out as they open and set aside.

When you judge the rice to be nearly ready, add the infused saffron, the prawn tails, clams and mussels. Add another ladle of stock and the parsley, and then stir carefully. Serve directly from the cooking pot.

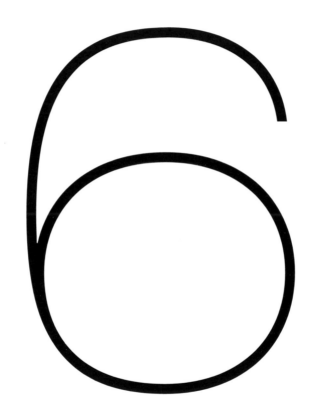

Carne

CARNE ALLA GRIGLIA
GRILLED MEATS

Throughout the vine-growing and olive-growing areas of Italy, the most popular form of meat cooking is over a wood fire. There is an obvious appeal in cooking over aromatic wood, the lure of the barbecue, and when it's done skilfully, with care and with good raw materials, the results are memorable. Unfortunately nine times out of ten in the Orvieto region, the results are disastrous: poor-quality, badly trimmed meat incinerated to resemble a leathery forensic exhibit.

The Fire
The primary concern with grilling meat is the fire itself: flames are a no-no, glowing red hot embers are the ticket. The heat used for grilling a very tender cut rare should be much fiercer (probably just as the initial flames have died down) than those needed to cook a chicken (a slow, steady, roasting glow). Barbecues need not have an even heat all over, colder spots are useful for resting meat. Some domestic barbecues allow you to raise and lower the grid, so this obviates the necessity of waiting for the fire to be exactly right: you merely move the food closer or further away from the heat.

Marinades and Seasoning
The Florentines believe that their beloved Val di Chiana beef steak needs absolutely nothing to enhance it except a vine wood fire: no salt, no pepper and no marinades. This is obsessively purist of them, a little bit of food snobbery well in line with their character. All meat, whatever quality, benefits from really quite copious seasoning with salt and pepper before grilling, the combination of wood flavours, seasoning and charring meat juices producing the wonderful exterior crust of properly barbecued food. I also prefer to brush meat with a flavoured oil before and, if necessary, during cooking.

Flavoured oil for grilling Take about 250 ml good olive oil and warm in a metal bowl on a corner of the barbecue. Tear up 2 bay leaves, strip the leaves from a large sprig of rosemary, and add these to the oil. Peel and chop 2 garlic cloves and add to the oil. A couple of chopped, seeded, small dried chillies make a good optional extra, as does a few sprigs of thyme or sage leaves.

How to Tell if Meat is Cooked
In the general guidelines given below all beef is grilled rare, lamb medium, and the rest well done. However, because barbecues and meat vary, the cooking times are of necessity approximate. There are a number of signs to indicate how done the meat is.

Rare When you press, the meat feels very soft, almost raw. A firm press with a finger will leave a dent the FBI could work with, and will not spring back. Larger cuts are more difficult to judge, but the larger the piece of meat the more accurate given cooking times tend to be. Remember that resting meat for a few minutes after grilling is essential, and that the meat continues to cook during this period usually advancing one degree of doneness, from blue to rare for example.

Medium Here the meat has firmed up. Pressing with your freshly washed digit will still produce a dent, but this will probably bead with red juices and then spring back. The red juices look as though the meat is still raw – wrong – it is definitely now medium.

Well done Meat will be firm and hardly take a finger dent at all. Juices will run out copiously and will either be clear or gravy coloured. Well-done meat, even beef, can be delicious but needs to be cooked over a slower fire, or it will dry.

Other grades Blue, medium well done, medium rare etc., etc., are all a nonsense, as the three stages above – red, pink and grey – are all you require, indeed all you can detect. If someone asks for blue they actually mean the meat must be raw and cold in the middle, a macho posturing.

What to Serve with Grilled Meat

French fries are hard to beat. A green salad certainly. Good quality potato crisps are something I've always particularly liked – the way they go soggy like game chips. Mustard, both English and Dijon, is essential and, like the Italians, a big wedge of lemon.

MANZO | BEEF

Fillet The tenderest cut of all and hideously expensive. Paying this much money, you have a right to demand and get the exact cut you want. Instead of grilling individual steaks, ask your butcher to trim a rump fillet for you to about 1 kg in weight, he needn't tie it. Season this cut very generously and brush with flavoured oil (see opposite). This needs cooking over a hot grill and when you have started, brush again with oil to urge the barbecue on. Do not turn or move the meat for 10 minutes then turn and give 10 minutes on the other side, brushing again with oil. You then need to rest the joint for 5 minutes and carve into 1 cm slices across the grain. The seasoning oil and oil-induced flames make for a wonderfully flavoured exterior which compensates for the slightly bland interior.

T-Bone Steak A seriously carnivorous cut which incorporates sirloin (fillet) and the bones between (incidentally containing spinal cord for BSE buffs). The definitive Bistecca alla Fiorentina is served at a trattoria in Florence called La Sostanza (or La Troia). Book a table and then be prepared for a long wait: the elderly irascible waiters will seat and serve every Italian in sight before they deign to recognise a tourist. Alternatively, turn up with a stunningly beautiful woman who speaks perfect Italian, and you will have a completely different experience. The loos at La Sostanza are only accessible by way of the kitchens. Discovering a weak bladder condition, several trips to the washroom became necessary before I had answered all my questions on the cooking methods used. Here are the results of that research.

The T-bones were at least 2 cm thick and often much more. They were seasoned just before grilling and brushed with a little oil then cooked over a very high heat (on a flimsy wire cake rack perched over an inferno). They were given about 8 minutes a side for the required 'rare' status and served with a lemon wedge – nothing else restrained carnality. Which brings me back to the above mentioned lady. She was scandalised when I tore into my steak bone using hand and fangs, and pointed out all the beautifully clad people in the room around me hacking away with knife and fork.

Sirloin Steak This has never been my favourite cut of beef, and only has great flavour when cooked in a large piece. For four people take 1 kg of boned (but not rolled) sirloin, and trim the fat down to a bare minimum. Season ultra-generously, brush with flavoured oil (see page 116), and grill for 10 minutes fat side down, then turn and give the other side 5 minutes. Rest over a cool part of the fire for 5 minutes then carve into 1 cm slices across the joint.

Rump Steak The classic British rump streak, huge and so attractive to compulsive meat-eaters, is a particularly poor cut for grilling. This is because it contains four different types of muscle tissue, each of which require markedly different amounts of cooking. There are two types of flank steak, one known as 'aiguillette' in French and the other in Britain as 'rump tail'. Both removed whole from a rump make marvellous little joints (about 600 g) for grilling. Continental butchers will sell these cuts, which also means that they will have the main part of the rump, the 'gluteus maximus' muscle, separated out and trimmed of the flavoursome but gristly top. (If your butcher will do this, try and utilise this small cut for a braise or stew.) The main muscle is a tasty, very lean cut, and sliced into large steaks would keep the Flintstones happy.

In general rump steak, be it flank or the central part, requires slower cooking than sirloin or fillet, but benefits from having a much stronger flavour.

Rib-eye Steak A classic British forerib needs trimming rather drastically before you can grill it. First get your butcher to chine and remove all bones except the ribs themselves – you will be paying for these bones so take them and freeze for stock. Then the coarse, grainy outer strip of meat and fat needs removing (this is good as boiled beef – try lightly salting it for two days like the Baccala on page 44, and then simmering slowly for 2 hours in a broth with carrot, onion, celery and leek). Now you are left with four or five ribs attached to a nicely marbled strip of rib-eye. Cut between the ribs to make four huge chops. Season and treat as T-bone, but it may need a few minutes' more cooking. These four chops will, when sliced up, serve eight, but you only have four bones to gnaw. Try and stop your friends fighting over them.

Skirt Steak or Flank Steak This cut is normally used for braising or stewing in Britain, and in fact is often called braising steak (*bavette* to French butchers). Grilled with panache and belligerence over a fierce heat, and sliced very rare, it is a wonderfully savoury but slightly chewy treat.

VITELLO | VEAL

Veal is like pork, not a very suitable meat for grilling, and it is expensive and very intolerant of sloppy cooking. Two parts of the animal can be grilled with great success – calves' liver (see page 129) and scallopini or veal escalopes. These latter should be sliced as thinly as possible, then bashed a little to tenderise and thin them further. Brush with oil, season lightly, and grill over a medium heat for 2 minutes on each side. Serve with Gremolata (see page 125) and a lemon wedge.

AGNELLO | LAMB

Lamb chops, whether best ends, loin or chump, are a natural for grilling, as they come in conveniently small pieces. The fire should be medium hot and you should try and get as much of the outside fat charred and rendered as possible. They require copious seasoning and a little oil before cooking. The rendering fat has a tendency to set the barbecue on fire, so long-handled tongs are vital. A French-trimmed rack of lamb grilled will take about 15 minutes on the fat side over a medium flame, and then 5 minutes on the flesh side followed by 5 minutes' rest before carving. Lamb should be grilled pink/medium, and benefits from herbs being scattered on it during cooking.

Cosce d'Agnello Disossate This butterflied leg of lamb is the best piece of lamb for grilling, and it will generously feed four or five people, providing both pink and well-done meat. Ask your butcher to bone and open out a small leg of lamb. He should then lightly flatten this out into an irregular rectangle with a few judicious taps of his mighty cleaver. Lay the meat flat in a high-sided tray and season very generously, then brush with flavoured oil (see page 116). Repeat on the other side. Leave to marinate at room temperature for 3–4 hours, loosely covered with a clean teatowel. This will at least partially age the meat, making up for modern butchers' inadequate hanging times. Scatter with extra rosemary.

The fire should be medium. Lift the meat out of its tray and without brushing off or draining the oil, slap it skin side down on the fire. The oil will probably blaze up at this stage, but this is all part of the ritual and is undeniably impressive. Grill without prodding or moving for 15 minutes then turn and cook for 5 minutes on the other non-fatty face. Now slide to a much cooler part of the grill, oil again and leave to calm down for 5 minutes.

Hack into chunks and serve with a green salad and pitta bread.

Fegatini (Lamb's Liver Faggots) Lamb is not my favourite type of liver, but from new season's lamb and very fresh, this is possibly the best way of cooking it. You will need to persuade your butcher to get you some caul fat (about 150 g), and to cut you 8 x 7–8 mm thick slices of best lamb's liver. This is for four people. Find 8 fine sage leaves and press one on to each slice, season lightly, cover and refrigerate the meat. Put the caul fat in a large bowl and rinse thoroughly for an hour under running water (careful, it has a habit of running over the edge of the bowl down the plughole and wreaking havoc in the 'U' bend). Spread the rinsed and drained caul fat out over a board and cut into 8 squares the size of this book. Wrap each slice of liver in this, pulling and stretching the caul as you go – it will surprise you how far it does stretch. This job is rather pleasant in an anatomical sort of way.

Season well and grill for 3 minutes on each side, then eat immediately, slightly pink. (My butcher in Italy prepares these for me, and they've converted me to the qualities of lamb's liver.)

MAIALE | PORK

Possibly the hardest of all meats to grill successfully because it really does need to be thoroughly cooked. This is not now a question of health, but of taste and digestibility. I only recommend you try the three ridiculously simple pork recipes – one with spare-ribs below, one with belly pork on page 134, and one with sausages on page 138.

Spare Ribs Buy 400 g per person, and demand that your butcher leaves them attached to each other in approximately 12 cm lengths. Put them in a pan of cold water and bring to the boil over a medium heat. Switch off and leave to cool in the water (about 1 hour). Drain the ribs and pat dry with kitchen roll. Season and brush liberally with flavoured oil (with all the chilli, thyme and sage options, see page 116). Allow to marinate while you get the barbecue going and it dies down to medium. Grill on each side until brown and crispy (approximately 15 minutes per side). These are very naturally flavoured ribs.

Pork Sausages Italian sausages cost a lot, but are worth every penny (or lira). They come in natural casings (skins) and on the barbecue at a medium heat they often burst and exude, providing little knobbly excrescences; these are crisp and radically good. If you insist on grilling British sausages, don't invite me!

Belly Pork On page 134 I give a recipe for roast belly pork. This is cooked on a rack in a roasting tin in the oven, but can be done over a low barbecue; it requires time, attention and possibly practice. Fortunately it is a cheap cut of meat and you can afford a dress rehearsal. The results are staggeringly good.

POLLO | CHICKEN

Chicken in the Orvieto region is an expensive meat. The birds are generally free-range, in fact strongly resemble the best-quality free-range French chickens (poulets de Bresse) in that they have genuine flavour, obvious maturity (they're big), and have well-developed legs without the over-large flaccid breasts of British poultry. They also come complete with every bit of them intact. Indeed butchers in Italy seem surprised when you ask them to clean the chicken. I imagine most Italian cooks are quite happy to do this job. Surprisingly, so are a large proportion of the guests at La Cacciata, in a volunteer class.

PICCIONE | SQUAB, DOVE OR DOMESTICATED PIGEON

Definitely not the Trafalgar Square variety, or a common or garden wood pigeon, but domesticated doves. The amount of dovecotes around Britain suggest that we once ate them regularly, but this is no longer the case, as all the ones restaurants serve are imported. Because the little beasts eat enormous amounts of grain in their short lives, yet obstinately refuse to get very fat, they are expensive to rear, and this price is passed on right up the food chain. The pigeons for my restaurants come from a beautiful estate near Grosetto on the Tuscan coastal plains.

For grilling purposes, unless you have a rotary spit, the birds need to be spatchcocked. Your butcher will do this for you, and if he doesn't know how, change butcher.

Lay the birds in a tray, brush with flavoured oil (see page 116), place a thin slice of lemon on each bird, then add salt and pepper. Turn the birds after an hour and repeat with oil and lemon, etc. Once you start to marinate the birds, do not refrigerate.

The point of spatchcocking is to render a near spherical object easy to grill by flattening it. Simply give the pigeons 8 minutes on the breast side and 5 minutes on the other. Rest in a warm part of the grill for 5 minutes more.

Try serving on Bruschetta (see page 104), with warm Grilled Mushrooms (see page 26) or with Rocket Salad (see page 38). Get your good Chianti out for this one.

Coda alla Vaccinara
Roman Oxtail

Literally 'oxtail in the leather-tanners' manner', more appetisingly known as the classic oxtail of Rome. The dominating flavours of oxtail, pancetta and red wine are tempered by lots of celery and the alien addition of a little bitter chocolate.

Pay particular attention to trimming the tails of all fat and constantly skimming during cooking. Several memorable versions of this dish in various restaurants in Rome have been spoilt by excessive greasiness. It is best to prepare the dish a day in advance and to refrigerate it overnight. Any greasy fat that has rendered out of the tails during cooking will float and set, and can easily be removed before reheating and serving.

4 people

1.5 kg oxtail, separated into its
    natural joints
plain flour
salt and pepper
good olive oil
100 g pancetta, cut into 5 mm dice
6 celery sticks, stringed and finely
    diced
3 medium carrots, peeled and
    finely diced
1 large onion, peeled and finely diced
1 garlic clove, peeled and minced
1 medium chilli pepper, seeded and
    minced
2 bay leaves
1/2 bottle red wine
125 g tinned tomato pieces
1 tsp cocoa powder or a tiny piece
    of bitter chocolate

Soak the oxtail pieces in cold water for 1 hour (at least). This will draw out some of the blood. Drain the oxtail, then dry and trim off as much external fat as you can. Season the flour by generously salting and peppering a plateful.

Heat a casserole with a little oil over a medium heat, then add the pancetta, half the celery, the carrot and the onion. Sweat for 10–15 minutes, taking care not to burn, and then add the garlic, chilli and bay leaves.

While this process is going on, with only the occasional prod or stir from you, heat a little oil in a large frying pan. Dredge the oxtail pieces in the seasoned flour then brown lightly and thoroughly over a medium flame on all sides. On no account burn the flour crust, it will spoil the taste of the whole dish. As and when the oxtail is browned, transfer to the casserole, then deglaze the frying pan by pouring in the red wine and boiling rapidly. Tip this into the casserole, then add the tomatoes and enough water to barely cover the meat. Stir thoroughly to ensure an even distribution of the chilli. Bring the casserole back to a simmer, turn the heat down to very low, then cover and simmer for 2 hours. Turn the meat once after an hour. When the 2 hours are up, allow to cool in the casserole and refrigerate overnight when completely cold.

The next day, or 1 hour before serving, scrape off any fat from the surface of the casserole. Bring the casserole back to a simmer (be careful that it does not scorch on the bottom). When simmering, add the remaining celery, then season cautiously and simmer very gently for an hour. About 5 minutes before serving add the cocoa. Stir in and check the seasoning. Turn the heat off and allow the meat to cool slightly before serving. It's great with chopped parsley mash (or rocket mash or garlic mash, see page 160).

Tagliata di Manzo con Funghi
Grilled Sliced Rib-eye Steak with Mushrooms

Il Setti Consuli is Orvieto's most serious restaurant: they are soberly and steadily setting their sights on gastronomic fame, Michelin stars etc. Despite this handicap, the cooking is good and the wine list spectacular. Tignanello 1989 was a very good year and used to feature on their wine list. I use the past tense because in the summer of 1994 I drank them out of it and the more expensive 1985. To accompany these liquid lunches, I ate this outstanding beef dish. Incidentally, I discovered that the meat was Aberdeen Angus and imported from Scotland.

2 people

500 g rib-eye steak in one piece
    (sirloin or rump will do)
300 g large ceps or cultivated
    mushrooms
salt and pepper
good olive oil

For the garlic butter:
225 g unsalted butter
juice of 1 lemon
1 handful parsley leaves
2 garlic cloves, peeled and minced

Make the garlic butter first. Allow the butter to soften. Squeeze the lemon juice into a bowl and add the soft butter in small pieces. Chop the parsley coarsely and add to the bowl along with the garlic, and season with salt and pepper. Stir and mash with a wooden spoon until mixed. Tip it out on to a large square of aluminium foil and roll into a tube 3 cm in diameter. Chill until needed.

Light your barbecue. I'm afraid a real fire is necessary for this dish. You need to cook your steak and mushrooms when the grill is very hot. Fan or blow on the fire just before cooking. Whilst the fire is dying down, season the meat copiously and lightly brush with olive oil. Do the same for the mushroom caps.

To grill the meat and mushrooms place the meat on the grill's hottest part and leave for 10 minutes. Arrange the mushroom caps topside down around the meat. Turn the mushrooms after 5 minutes and give 5 minutes on the other side, then remove to a tray or dish and keep slightly warm.

After 10 minutes turn the beef and give 10 minutes on the other side. This will be rare. Remove to the same tray as the mushrooms and rest for 10 minutes near enough to the fire to keep warm.

While the beef is resting, cut 4 x 1 cm slices of the garlic butter, and put these on top to melt and mingle with the beef and mushroom juices. Heat two dinner plates.

To serve, carve the steak into six angled slices, and arrange three on each plate. Cover these with half the mushrooms each, and pour over the juices. The dish will be at this stage lukewarm, this is intended. It is not meant to be hot; in many cases lukewarm or room-temperature food is better than hot.

Osso Buco con Piselli
Osso Buco with Peas

This is a springtime variant on the classic Osso Buco in Bianco. The Italians refer to any dish without tomatoes in it as 'in bianco'; presumably the jet black Risotto Nero of Venice is also white by this curious piece of culinary nomenclature. What it does is stress the importance of tomatoes in Italian cooking, in that they are conspicuous by their absence.

Veal is a highly emotive subject. Tender pale-pink Dutch or Lombardy veal makes wonderful roasts or, as scaloppini, provides one of the mainstays of Italian meat cookery. Unfortunately calves are reared in conditions of unspeakable cruelty, so cruel that such rearing is illegal in Great Britain. The alternative is vitellone – the meat of male calves that are reared normally, weaned, fed on grass and then killed. This is much more humane, but dubious gastronomically, as it represents a halfway stage between veal and beef, and misses most of the good points of each. To roast or quickly cook this older darker meat is impractical – it is simply too tough – but it can be braised with considerable success.

The veal generally available around Orvieto is vitellone, and this influences the dishes taught at the school. We go for the slow-cooked dishes such as Lo Stinco (see page 128) or this wonderful osso buco. Incidentally, the creation of crate-fed veal is the by-product of our demand for milk products. Milk farmers necessarily have large quantities of male calves surplus to requirements, and flog them to Holland via Brightlingsea. Cattle that produce good milk yields are generally not very good at producing the beef that our meat industry deems good for us, hence the need to get rid of it as calves. As we in Britain eat very little veal, perhaps the best solution would be to find or develop a breed of cattle which can satisfy both the dairy and beef industry needs.

If you wish to cook this dish, but don't wish to buy crate-fed veal, seek out an organic or cruelty-free butcher and he will advise you, but remember it will be expensive. Osso buco is cut from the shin, an extremity, which should be relatively cheap, but an overwhelming demand from restaurants has forced the price up.

4 people

4 slices osso buco, 4–5 cm thick and about 300 g each
sunflower oil
salt and pepper
2 medium carrots, 3 celery sticks, 2 onions, all peeled and finely diced for soffritto
1 bottle dry white wine
2 bay leaves, 6 parsley stalks and 1 sprig of thyme, tied into a bouquet garni

You will need an ovenproof casserole big enough to hold the meat snugly, preferably in one layer, and a large frying pan. Set the oven to 180°C/350°F/Gas 4.

Heat a little sunflower oil in the frying pan over a medium flame. Season the meat copiously and brown for 5 minutes on one side then turn and repeat. Transfer this meat to the casserole. Tip the prepared soffritto into the frying pan and sauté, slightly browning. Add this to the casserole, then pour the white wine into the frying pan, turn up the heat and boil. Scrape any brown stuck pieces of meat or vegetable off the pan. Tip the wine into the casserole (if using a black iron pan, wash and dry immediately after use as the wine seems to

1 kg fresh peas in pod, podded (freeze the pods for Vegetable Broth)

**For the Gremolata
(prepare just before serving):**
1 handful picked parsley leaves
1 garlic clove, peeled
1 lemon

promote rust). Put the casserole over a medium heat and add the bouquet garni and enough water to barely cover the meat. Bring to a simmer, stir and cover, then transfer to the preheated oven. Braise for 2 hours and then check for doneness: if the meat is correctly cooked, it should be beginning to detach itself from the bone but not be completely separated. It may need another half hour.

The dish can be prepared in advance up to this point, indeed benefits from being cooked the day before. However, if you do this, allow to cool completely, remove the meat very carefully with a slotted spoon, wrap in clingfilm, then refrigerate. Transfer the sauce to a clean container and refrigerate separately.

If made the day before, remove the sauce from the fridge and scrape off any fat. Transfer back to the casserole. If making as a continuous process, simply but carefully remove the meat and skim. Add the peas and simmer over a medium heat until the peas are done. This will take a surprisingly long time – up to 40 minutes – and the sauce will reduce and intensify in the process. Check seasoning, return the meat to the casserole, cover and heat through in the oven (the same temperature as before) for 15 minutes or very slowly on a medium to low flame.

While the casserole is reheating make the gremolata. Coarsely chop the parsley. Mince the garlic and add it to the parsley. Grate the lemon zest through the Parmesan hole of a cheese grater and add to the parsley and garlic. Mix thoroughly to avoid serving all the garlic to one guest.

Preheat four large soup plates. Uncover the casserole and skim away any excess fat – carefully, because the osso buco are very fragile. Lift out each piece of meat on to a plate. Ladle over the liquor and vegetables, then sprinkle with the gremolata. Serve with mashed potatoes (see page 160). Do not tell your guests how delicious the marrow is, then you can sneakily eat it all in the kitchen when they leave it!

Vitello Arrosto
Roast Veal

Marcella Hazan deserves the blame for addicting me to Italian cooking and through that to Italy itself. Many of the recipes in this book were introduced to me by her marvellous *Classic Italian Cooking* nearly twenty years ago. This one is perhaps the most memorable. I was sitting reading it in a small cafe in Firenze waiting for my companion to finish shopping, when the logic and simplicity of the recipe caught my imagination. The city was ransacked for Vitello Arrosto: many trattorie were tried, but all were found wanting. Then on the autostrada to Roma, we stopped at an Agip motorway caff, and on the blackboard: Vitello Arrosto. It was precisely as the blessed Marcella described it – a whole rump, meltingly savoury, brown exterior and possibly ever so slightly pink in the middle. There was no gravy, just the meat, some OK roast potatoes and spinach, it was bliss.

The precise cut to use for this method of roasting is important, as it will only work with prime cuts and it will only work with veal, not vitellone (see page 124). I have used a best-end here, trimmed like a rack, which will feed six people. The best alternative is a whole rump, which will be more expensive and will feed eight, maybe more. Any leftovers are wonderful the next day as sandwiches, and of course there is always vitello tonnato, using the tuna sauce on page 144.

Ask your butcher to chine the meat, leaving just the four or five ribs attached. He should also French trim the ribs and chop all bones and trimmings for you. In short the veal is like a very big rack of lamb. The trimmings can be used next time you make broth.

6 people
1 best end of veal, trimmed
    (see above)
salt and pepper
good olive oil
1/2 bottle dry white wine
1 sprig rosemary
lemons to garnish

Preheat the oven to 180°C/350°F/Gas 4. You will need a deep-sided casserole into which the meat fits relatively snugly.

Season the veal generously. Heat the casserole with a little oil over a medium flame, then brown the veal thoroughly on all faces. This process is vital and should take up to 15 minutes. When the veal is well sealed, turn it on its back so the bones are downwards and forming a natural roasting rack. Add 2 glasses of white wine: it will bubble and spit a little. Baste the meat well and put uncovered in the oven with the rosemary. Roast for 15 minutes then baste again and give another 15 minutes. Repeat for a final quarter of an hour, basting again. As the wine evaporates, add the remaining wine and, towards the end if necessary, a little water.

Plan A

The Italians would simply serve the veal from the casserole with the rather concentrated brown juices remaining in the pan. I think this is probably the best way, so simply take the roast out of the oven, turn it a few times, covering the upperside in the juices. Leave in a warm place to rest for 10 minutes, then carve, scraping a little caramelised juice over each slice. You should be able to get one slice with rib followed by one slice cut from between the ribs and so on.

Plan B

If you think your guests would like or expect a gravy then remove the veal to a heated dish, transfer the casserole to a medium flame and add 2 wine glasses of water. With a wooden spoon stir and scrape as you deglaze the casserole. Boil the resulting juices until you consider it tasty enough, then add about 50 g butter in pieces, swirling it in off the heat. If you insist on thickening the gravy, use 2 tsp potato flour dissolved in the same amount of water.

You may notice a generic resemblance between this recipe and the Maiale al Latte (see page 136). One uses wine and the other uses milk, but the method of cooking and the cut of meat are remarkably similar, they are in fact interchangeable.

Lo Stinco
Poached White Shin of Veal

Instead of cutting a shin of veal into slices for osso buco, here it is first poached to half tenderness then braised in the reduced cooking liquor with vegetables and wine. This is a lengthy and troublesome dish to make – stretched over two days – but gives an undeniably spectacular result.

6–8 people

For the poaching:

2 shins of veal on the bone

5 kg veal bones, chopped into
    4 cm pieces (ask your butcher
    to do this)

4 celery sticks, coarsely chopped

4 carrots, coarsely chopped

4 onions, peeled and coarsely
    chopped

good olive oil

For the braising:

4 carrots, peeled and cut into
    5 mm dice

6 onions, peeled and cut into
    5 mm dice

1 celeriac, peeled and cut into
    5 mm dice

2 bay leaves

1 bottle red wine

Little **Tip**

■ Remove the shins to a chopping board and carve. You do this by grasping the protruding bone and slicing the meat vertically – lay these slices on the serving dish. Coat with a little sauce and vegetables. Very, very good with Braised Fagioli and Pancetta or Sautéed Swiss Chard (see page 164).

Poaching the veal (day one)

Preheat the oven to its maximum. Put the chopped veal bones and chopped vegetables into a lightly oiled roasting dish and brown thoroughly in the oven, for 40 minutes approximately.

Take a large stockpot and pile the browned bones and vegetables in it. Put the shins of veal on top. Cover with cold water and bring slowly to the boil. Turn down the heat to the barest simmer and skim thoroughly. Simmer for 2 hours, skimming occasionally, then remove the veal shins and cool. Clingfilm these and refrigerate. Continue cooking the stock gently for 4 more hours, then sieve into a medium pan. Throw away the vegetables and bones, and return the stock to the boil. Skim thoroughly as it returns to the boil. Continue boiling rapidly until the stock is reduced by half. Allow to cool, then refrigerate. Congratulations, you have just made veal stock!

Braising the veal (day two)

You will need a deep casserole or roasting dish big enough to hold the veal shins, vegetables and stock.

Preheat the oven to 180°/350°F/Gas 4. Lightly oil your casserole and add the prepared vegetables and bay leaves. Brown lightly for 10 minutes. Add the red wine and boil, then place the veal shins on their sides on the bed of vegetables. Add enough of the stock to half cover the meat. Baste the meat as you do this. Put the casserole in the oven and cook, uncovered, for 1 hour, basting and turning often. If the stock level falls dramatically, add more, but never more than halfway up the shins.

Very carefully remove the shins to your serving dish and keep warm. Bring the liquid and vegetables in the casserole to a boil and reduce until slightly syrupy.

Check the seasoning. Spoon some of the braised vegetables around the meat, and serve the rest separately. Baste the meat with a little stock and keep the rest on the side for serving. Present to your guests to gasps of admiration.

Fegato alla Veneziana
Calves' Liver and Onions in the Venetian Style

Disregarding considerations of cruelty and humane animal husbandry, the innards of veal calves make some of the finest meat dishes. Sweetbreads, brains, testicles and the tripes are all wonderful, particularly the Roman speciality of Pagliata, the small intestine still full of milky substances which I thought a nauseating concept until I inadvertently tried it.

Of all the veal 'variety meats' ('American speak' for offal), liver is possibly the finest, and certainly the most likely to be appreciated by the majority of your guests. Calves' liver is pale, tender and mild in flavour; it frequently converts liver-haters to its cause, but is rather expensive. You may have to search for it or bully your butcher to order it for you.

Ask your butcher to trim and slice it thinly; you will need approximately 125–150 g per person. The butcher will probably leave the outer skin on each slice. (This helps the meat remain firm when slicing, allowing larger thinner slices.) But ask him to remove the skin after he's cut the slices; it's an unpleasant task.

The classic Italian liver dish best known outside Italy is Fegato alla Veneziana or liver and onions. This marriage is one made in heaven, it can't be bettered, and like all the best liaisons does not brook tampering or interference. The secret to cooking the liver is to keep the cooking brief, and not to cook it too fiercely because when the surface scorches it has an unpleasant taste and rather rank charred odour.

4 people

500 g calves' liver, thinly sliced and skinned
salt and pepper
35 g butter
a little good olive oil
500 g onions, peeled and finely sliced
4 sage leaves
a handful of chopped parsley
2 lemons, halved

You will need a large frying pan. Cut the liver into ribbons 5–6 cm long and 5 mm across. Season the liver generously. Take a large frying pan and melt half the butter with a little oil over a medium heat. Add the onions and sage, stir and turn down the heat, then allow the onion to soften and go translucent over 15 minutes or so with the sage leaves. Turn the heat up to medium and add the liver. Cook, occasionally turning the liver, for 4–5 minutes until the liver has stiffened slightly and coloured. Throw in the remaining butter and add the parsley. Check the seasoning and serve with lemon halves. Delicious with mashed potatoes or wet polenta.

129

Fegato alla Marsala
Calves' Liver with Marsala

A Sicilian calves' liver dish using the sweet wine from the island, but with a heretical addition of a little good-quality red wine vinegar to balance its sweetness.

4 people
500 g calves' liver in 4 good slices,
    trimmed and skinned
a little good olive oil
salt and pepper
6 tbsp Marsala wine
1 tbsp red wine vinegar
35 g butter

Heat a frying pan big enough to hold the liver in one layer over a medium flame. Add a little olive oil, season the liver and cook on one side for 3 minutes. Turn and give the other side 2 minutes. You may not have a frying pan large enough to hold the liver in one go, in which case cook in two batches keeping the first warm in a 110°C/225°/F/Gas 1/4 oven. Wipe the pan after the first batch, and add more oil. (Saves washing-up!)

Remove the liver from the pan and transfer to a warm serving plate. Add the Marsala and vinegar to the pan, turn up the flame and boil down until syrupy. At this point add the butter in pieces, off the heat, then shake the pan until the butter is incorporated into the sauce. Pour over the liver and serve. The whole process of making the sauce should only take a minute or so.

Fegato alla Griglia
Barbecued Grilled Liver

This is the simplest way to cook liver. One danger is that the burnt taste of the charred stripes will overwhelm the liver's delicate flavour.

I like grilled calves' liver with English mustard. Incidentally, the Italians don't eat much mustard, and if you want to get some in a restaurant ask for 'senape' (stress on the last e). Repeated demands by me for 'mostarda' in a posh Roman restaurant met with slack-jawed incomprehension from the waiter until my companion tried 'senape' (in her native Danish). Instant success, the lights went on behind his eyes and off he ran to the delicatessen to get us some.

500 g calves' liver in 4 good slices,
    trimmed and skinned
good olive oil
salt and pepper
8 slices smoked pancetta or good-
    quality bacon (optional)
2 lemons halved

If barbecuing, allow the fire to die down. If using a ridged grill pan, heat to medium. Marinate the liver in a little olive oil with salt and pepper while you get everything else ready. If using the pancetta, grill this in advance and keep warm (wipe grill pan if using).

Grill the liver for 2–3 minutes on the first side. Do not attempt to move it until it is time for turning. Grill for 2 minutes on the other side. Serve with the grilled pancetta and lemon halves.

Agnello Arrosto
Roast Lamb

Most Italian roasting has evolved from a form of cooking not unlike pot-roasting: the meat never went near the oven, indeed until relatively recently few Italian homes had ovens. Meat was typically browned in a casserole, various flavourings were added, it was moistened with wine, and then cooked over a medium to low heat, and basted regularly. With the exception of veal, meat is nearly always very well done.

This lamb recipe follows this method, but places the meat uncovered in an oven. Accompany with Roast Potatoes with Vinegar, Garlic and Rosemary (see page 160) or the Salad of Roasted Vegetables (see page 36).

4–6 people
1 small leg of lamb
good olive oil
salt and pepper
1 sprig rosemary
2 bay leaves
1 sprig thyme
1/2 bottle wine (red or white)
500 ml Chicken Broth
    (see page 186)

You will need an oval casserole or roasting dish not much bigger than the joint, and a suitably sized ovenproof serving dish. Preheat the oven to 200°C/400°F/Gas 6.

Rub the lamb with olive oil and season it copiously. Put the lamb in the roasting dish, skin side up, add the herbs and put in the oven, adding a little extra olive oil. After 15 minutes turn the lamb and moisten with a glass of wine. Return to the oven for 15 minutes. Turn the lamb again and remoisten with more wine. Roast for 15 minutes more, turn and then repeat the process for one final time with the rest of the wine. The lamb has now had an hour. Transfer to the ovenproof serving dish. Moisten with olive oil and return to the oven which you should then switch off.

Reduce the wine and juices in the roasting dish, and add the broth, then boil vigorously until syrupy.

Remove the lamb from the oven, pour any juices into the reduced wine in the roasting dish and sieve this gravy into a sauceboat. Carve the lamb as normal, then serve with the sauce. This recipe is particularly good done with lamb shanks or a shoulder; both will typically need an extra half an hour.

Arista alla Fiorentina
Roast Loin of Pork Florentine Style

The food of Florence is characterised by simplicity and elegance and, above all, quality of ingredients. The Florentines make the English seem positively fancy in their desire to leave food 'un-mucked about with'. This dish uses three ingredients which are readily and superbly available at La Cacciata: free-range pork, rosemary (a large bush outside the kitchen door) and, of course, the Belcapos' Umbrian nectar, extra virgin olive oil.

The toxic waste-product passed off as pork in Britain will not do for this dish – you must find free-range pork which has ample fat (some 2 cm between skin and flesh). This fat is removed and not served here, but its presence is felt in the roasting quality of the meat. (Keep the skin and fat and freeze it to use as crackling in the future.) The rack or rib end of the loin is essential as well – this is sometimes known as the best end.

Potatoes are roasted around the joint, do not omit them. In fact don't tamper with this recipe in any way, or you will be missing a uniquely Italian taste.

4–6 people

1 rack of pork, approx. 1.25 kg,
    with the skin and most of the
    fat removed
2 sprigs rosemary
1 garlic clove, peeled
sea salt and black pepper
6 tbsp extra virgin olive oil
1 kg new potatoes, peeled

Bone the pork with a strong serrated knife, carefully cutting between the meat and the ribs until you run into the chine bone. Do this slowly, sawing gently, and pulling the meat away from the bone. When you reach the bottom of the ribs you must turn the knife through 90 degrees and remove the chine bones. It is important that you do this with the meat and bones in two separate pieces but no more. This sounds much more difficult than it is. If you leave too much meat on the bones it doesn't matter because the two separate pieces are reunited with a rosemary stuffing before roasting. If you can't face this procedure take this book to your butcher and get him to do it!

For the rosemary stuffing and assembly of the pork, strip the rosemary needles from the stem and chop finely with the clove of garlic. Season with sea salt and abundant black pepper, milled fairly coarsely. Bind this mixture with 1–2 tbsp of olive oil and spread it on the inside surfaces of the ribs and chine piece where the main body of the meat has been removed. Replace the meat and tie securely between each rib to reassemble the joint.

Again if you find this whole performance a bad idea, make the stuffing and take it to your butcher and mime it out for him or show him the recipe. (Butchers all over the country are going to be cursing my name!)

Season the outside of the pork generously. The pork will benefit from being prepared and stuffed the day before; the relatively large amount of seasoning will partially cure the meat and bring up the flavour.

Dice the potatoes into large bite-sized pieces, then season and dress with a little olive oil. Preheat the oven to 180°C/350°F/Gas 4.

To cook the meat, take a roasting dish big enough to hold the potatoes and roast in a single layer, and lightly oil it with extra virgin olive oil. Put the roast in, resting it on the ribs (which form a natural trivet or rack, and allow the fat from the roast to drip off and fry the potatoes without over-browning the meat). Strew the potatoes around the roast and sprinkle everything with more olive oil. Roast for 1 1/2 hours, turning the oven down to 160°C/325°F/Gas 3 after half an hour. Do not touch until this half an hour has elapsed, then remove the dish from the oven and turn the potatoes. Repeat this procedure after another half hour. The roast now needs yet another half hour.

When the roast is done (check by inserting a skewer for 5 seconds, and then clear juices should bubble up out of the hole), switch off the oven and remove the dish. Transfer the potatoes to a separate serving dish, and keep hot in the switched-off oven. Allow the pork to rest in a warm place.

To carve, snip the strings and remove the meat roll from the bones. Cut this into 1 cm slices and arrange on a platter. Serve with the potatoes and a few sprigs of fresh rosemary (possibly some spinach, see page 164). Hack and separate all the bones and serve with fingerbowls after the first part of the meat is eaten. The meat on the bones is quite superb and can redefine FHB ('family hold back'). The staff at La Cacciata pester me to give the loan meat to the clients and the bones to them. They would, wouldn't they, being either Italian or Italianised. Of course they don't get the bones, I save them for myself…

Panna di Maiale Arrosto
Roast Belly of Pork

A rather off-putting title in English and if you make it with a normal piece of British pork, an off-putting dish. Pork husbandry in Britain is by and large a disgrace: the animals are reared squalidly and cruelly for a very short time, and they all too soon become carcasses that are the result of a conspiracy between bacon producers and food faddists, with lean and unpalatable meat. What pigs need to do is root around, find their own food (supplemented with swill) and end up with at least 2 cm fat between skin and flesh. Lean pork is an abomination, and I pronounce my gastronomic fatwa on the producers of lean pork: may they live forever more in Muslim countries. The Italians know all about pork, and have done for 2,000 years since the Gauls taught them under duress to make hams.

For this recipe you want pork belly with at least 2 cm fat between skin and flesh. The ribs should still be in place. Ask your butcher to cut it into two pieces.

8 people
1 belly of pork (see above),
    approx. 2 kg
sea salt
black pepper
fresh rosemary

You will need a roasting tin with a rack. Preheat the oven to 200°C/400°F/Gas 6.

With a roasting fork jab the meat on the skin side very thoroughly. This will allow the fat below the skin to seep through as it renders out and ensure amazing crackling. Sprinkle the meat lavishly with sea salt and pepper and place, skin side up, on the rack. Roast for 2 hours, turning the oven down to 150°C/300°F/Gas 2 after half an hour. You do not baste, you do not turn the meat. If you wish to reserve the copious amounts of fat rendered, pour them out of the dish now and then.

If after 2 hours the skin is not completely crackling, cook briefly under an overhead grill. If during the cooking it seems to be burning, turn the oven down more, and very loosely cover with a sheet of foil. (If you tightly cover it, steam will be generated and the crackling will go down the tubes.) When the pork is done, allow to sit in the switched-off oven for 20 minutes to relax.

Spear the roast with a fork, and transfer to a large carving board. Turn over and carve with a serrated knife, sawing firmly and energetically when you reach the crackling. The ribs will indicate where you should cut, i.e. between them. Serve on a big plate with any juices that have accumulated in the roasting pan while the meat was resting and also any carving juices.

This dish forms a natural partnership with Red Cabbage (see page 165). Cold, the meat is delicious sliced in sandwiches, or served with mustard and green salad.

Maiale al Latte
Pork Cooked in Milk

In the spring of 1995 I went to Ballymaloe House near Cork in Ireland to do a guest chef stint at Darina Allen's cookery school there. Legendary Irish hospitality made for a wonderful week, and perhaps the most hospitable act was to slaughter one of their hand-raised pigs for me to do this recipe. Sounds gruesome, but you had to be there to taste the result. Darina said it was the best pork dish she had ever tasted and modestly I had to agree with her, stating the obvious that it was also the best pork I'd ever had a chance to cook.

If you want to cook this dish go and find some free-range or organically reared pork with at least 2 cm fat between skin and meat. The preferred cut is best end of the loin which you should ask your butcher to chine and skin; make sure he gives you the chopped up chine bones and the skin to make crackling. Ask him to leave approximately half the fat on the roast and half attached to the skin. The rib bones should still be attached to the joint and the roasting is done with these under the meat forming a kind of rack. Do not omit the marination; some authorities do and they are missing a vital step. The interaction between the pork, the marinade and some complex enzyme action in the cooked milk is what produces the exceptionally tender and moist result.

4–6 people

1.25 kg best end loin of pork,
    prepared as above
salt and pepper
3 tbsp cider vinegar
300 ml dry white wine
3 tbsp olive oil
at least 1 litre full cream milk
1 sprig rosemary

For the marination, season the pork and put it to marinate in the vinegar and wine for at least 2 hours, preferably more.

To roast, preheat the oven to 180°C/350°F/Gas 4. Remove the pork from the marinade, pat dry and season a little more. Put the olive oil in a suitably sized roasting dish or casserole, heat over a medium flame, then add the pork and brown it as uniformly as possible. Add the chine bones and the marinade and transfer to the oven for 15 minutes, making sure that the joint is perched on its bones rather than fat side down.

After this 15 minutes the marinade should have nearly evaporated, so add 500 ml of the milk and the rosemary. It will almost immediately boil. As soon as this subsides a little, baste the meat generously and return to the oven. Turn the oven down to 150°C/300°F/Gas 2, and roast uncovered for a further 1 1/4 hours, basting with the milk as often as you can. If the milk is showing signs of drying up add a little more.

Test the joint for doneness by inserting a cooking fork for 10 seconds then withdrawing it and gingerly touching the part of the tines which were in the centre of the meat to your lips. Cooked meat is hot but not scalding (you hope). If you have any doubts, baste the meat and give another 15 minutes – nobody in their right mind likes rare pork.

To finish, remove the pork from the oven and take it out of the roasting dish. Rest on a serving platter in a warm place (perhaps the switched-off oven). Examine the rather unappetising mess in the roasting tray. If rather dry and brown with blobs of cooked milk, add 500 ml water and boil, stirring vigorously, until a recognisable gravy is formed, then pass through a sieve into a small pan and simmer slowly until needed. If on the other hand there is copious liquid, simply boil everything down to concentrate it and sieve as above. The first option is the more likely: as you have been roasting everything uncovered, so extensive evaporation will have taken place.

To carve, remove the serving plate from the heat and transfer the pork to a carving board. Pour or scrape any juices from the plate into the gravy. Cut the pork into slices between the ribs, one slice with a rib, one slice without, and arrange on the hot serving plate. Pour any juices from the chopping board into the gravy and coat the pork with it. Serve with crackling, if done, and the rest of the gravy in a sauce boat.

This joint is very good with boiled new potatoes and sautéed Swiss chard (or spinach).

Crackling

Prick the skin very, very thoroughly all over with a cooking fork or small sharp knife. Rub thoroughly with salt and roast on a rack with the joint. The fat should bubble through the holes and crisp the skin. If not quite crisp enough at the end of the pork's cooking time, transfer the crackling to under a low grill; this will finish it in record time.

SALSICCE | SAUSAGES

Fresh Italian sausages are wonderful, fresh British sausages are vile, this is a law of nature. My butcher, Donato, at the nearby village of Porano, makes sausages to order, and will discuss your specifications. His shop may not meet all modern EU health regulations, indeed often resembles the carnage of a battlefield, but the meat is wonderful.

Italian delicatessens sometimes make their own sausages or sell them vacuum-packed from Italy. Look out for the 'piccante' (spicy) ones.

Salsicce e Peperoni
Sausages and Peppers

In this recipe, the sausages are roasted then slathered with onions and roasted peppers. You will need to make the Insalata di Peperoni (see page 34) before attempting the dish.

I was inspired to cook this by Calvin Trillan's description in one of his excellent *Let's Eat* Trilogy. He writes of these pepper, onion and sausage sandwiches served at the Feast of San Gennaro in New York's Little Italy. He thinks he tried 43 sausages over the weekend – just the sort of dedication to greed I admire. This is my version.

4–6 people

500 g–700 g Italian sausages (Luganega are one type), preferably spicy

1 recipe Insalata di Peperoni (see page 34)

good olive oil

4 large onions, peeled and cut into rings

salt and pepper

Preheat the oven to 180°C/350°F/Gas 4. Remove the strings from the sausages (if present). Oil a frying pan or roasting dish big enough to hold the sausages. Moisten with a little water, arrange the bangers in it and fry or roast for 20 minutes, turning occasionally.

Take a large frying pan and heat 4 tbsp olive oil over a medium heat. Add the onions and brown them steadily whilst the sausages are cooking. Bring the peppers to room temperature.

When the sausages have had 20 minutes, remove from the oven and add the peppers and onions, season, toss and return to the oven for 15 minutes. Allow to cool slightly before serving.

Try serving this dish with ciabatta and incite your guests to make Italian hot-dogs. Incidentally the whole dish can be made successfully on a barbecue.

SALSICCE CON LENTICCHE | SAUSAGES AND LENTILS
Cook the sausages as in the recipe for Salsicce e Peperoni, and serve with their fat poured over a bowl of plainly cooked Italian green lentils. Serve with mustard.

COTECHINO
A large boiling sausage made with quite large amounts of pork rind minced into it (this is one of the reasons why most pork is sold skinless in Italy). Available in packets in England, simmer in their foil envelopes for 1 hour (do not boil). Slit the envelope carefully (the edges are razor sharp), and serve with the juices over lentils or the Fagioli di Toscana on page 164.

ZAMPONE
The same sausage mixture as cotechino, but stuffed in a boned pig's trotter. Freshly made, these are one of the gastronomic wonders of the world; even industrially produced ones are great. Serve as cotechino. Delicious in a cassoulet or bollito misto.

Pollo Orvietano
Orvieto Chicken

Undoubtedly (at least to me) one of the greatest chicken dishes of the world. You should only attempt this if you can get copious quantities of leaf or feather fennel (all you herb gardeners). Bronze fennel will do.

4–6 people

1 x 1.5–2 kg free-range or corn-
    fed chicken
good olive oil
500 g chicken livers, cleaned and
    diced
2 large potatoes, peeled and cut
    into 1 cm dice
1 enormous bunch leaf or feather
    fennel (ask smart greengrocers
    for imported wild fennel)
48 black olives, stoned (yes,
    how boring!)
salt and pepper
48 large fresh garlic cloves in
    their skins
250 ml dry white wine
500 ml Chicken Broth (see page 186)

The stuffing takes a minimum of an hour, including cooling time, and is best done in advance. Put 4 tbsp olive oil to heat over a medium flame in a frying pan, add the livers and stir until coloured. Then add the diced potatoes, and cook until they are tender (you may need to add more oil, as the potatoes will stick, but don't worry, simply scrape the crispy bits into the mixture). It is important that the potatoes are fully cooked. Coarsely chop half the fennel and add to the potatoes with half the olives. Mix thoroughly, season with salt and pepper, and set aside to cool.

Preheat the oven to 200°C/400°F/Gas 6.

Spoon the cool stuffing into the chicken. You will have quite a lot left. Rub the chicken all over with olive oil, and season very generously. Put the remaining stuffing in a suitably sized gratin dish with a little olive oil and set aside.

Put the chicken on its side into a casserole, and roast in the oven for 20 minutes, uncovered. It should be spitting and generally furious by this time. Gingerly turn the chicken on to the other side, and give it 20 minutes more; turn down the oven to 180°C/350°F/Gas 4 if it is browning too much. Put the excess stuffing into the oven to roast. Add the garlic cloves to the casserole and turn the chicken, breast side down, for 20 minutes. Turn it breast up, add the remaining fennel and olives and roast for a further 10-15 minutes.

Remove the fowl from the casserole to the chopping board and let it rest. Keep the garlic and olives warm in a dish. Remove any excess fat from the casserole. Add the wine to the casserole and boil vigorously until nearly evaporated. Add the broth and reduce by three-quarters. This whole process should take 10 minutes.

Cut the chicken into eighths, and arrange on a heated serving platter around the scooped-out stuffing. Scatter more chopped fennel, the olives and garlic on top, and serve with extra stuffing.

Pollo alla Griglia
Grilled Chicken

4–6 people
1 x 1.25–1.5 kg free-range chicken

For the marinade:
100 ml good olive oil
100 g Dijon style mustard
2 garlic cloves, peeled
1 handful parsley leaves
juice of 2 lemons
coarse black pepper
sea salt

If you haven't got a spit rôtisserie attachment on your barbecue, ask your butcher to split and flatten the chicken into two, then proceed as below.

Put all the marinade ingredients into a food processor and whirl to a paste. Paint over the chicken and leave to sit for 2–3 hours. Skewer and roast the chicken for 50 minutes, taking care that the skin does not char too much. Check for doneness by puncturing a thigh: if the juices run clearly and copiously, then the bird is ready for its pre-carving siesta. Move the carcass to a cooler place for 10 minutes' rest. If the juices run pink, roast for 10 minutes more.

If grilling the halved chicken, you will need a fairly slow fire. Give 15 minutes with the skin side down, then 10 minutes on the other. Pull the breasts away from the legs and set aside on a much cooler part of the fire. The legs will require longer, a further 10 minutes at least.

Insalata di Cappone
Capon Salad

The title is a misnomer in that it is no longer possible to buy capons, and this is as true in Italy as here.

8 people
1 x 2.5 kg poached chicken (see page 187)
250 g pine nuts, toasted lightly
sea salt
top-quality olive oil
a handful of parsley leaves

For the dressing:
250 ml red wine vinegar
2 bay leaves
2 tbsp caster sugar
1 cinnamon stick
1/2 tsp ground black pepper
150 g raisins
zest of 1 orange and 1 lemon, in strips

For the dressing put the vinegar in a pan and bring to the boil, then add the bay leaves, sugar, cinnamon, pepper, raisins and zests. Stir until the sugar is dissolved and leave over a very low heat to infuse.

Shred the chicken meat into a large bowl discarding all skin, fat and bone. This is a messy but easy job. Add the pine nuts to the chicken. Return the vinegar mix to the boil, picking out the bay leaves and cinnamon. Pour this mix over the chicken, season with sea salt, and toss thoroughly. The liquid will nearly all be absorbed by the meat. The salad can now be kept refrigerated for up to 3 days; the flavours may even be said to improve.

To serve, remove the salad from the fridge at least an hour before serving. Add olive oil to taste (about 200 ml). Add the parsley leaves and toss.

Coniglio con Salvia
Rabbit with Sage

This is a very useful recipe in that it can become two dishes. As detailed here, you have a delicious braised rabbit. With the rabbit boned and diced after cooking, it becomes the classic Tuscan Sugo di Coniglio, paired with pappardelle (see page 75).

4 people
1 rabbit, weighing 1.5-2 kg, cut into 8
　　pieces (ask your butcher to do this)
good olive oil
salt and pepper
150 g pancetta, cut into 5 mm dice
1 onion, 2 carrots, 1 celery stick, all
　　peeled and finely diced for sofritto
250 ml tinned tomato pieces
150 ml white wine
2 bay leaves
1 bunch sage

Heat a little olive oil in a large frying pan. Season the rabbit pieces and brown thoroughly over a medium flame, about 10 minutes, turning regularly.

While the rabbit is browning, sweat the pancetta in a large casserole. When it renders a little fat, add the sofritto and sweat for 10 minutes. Add the tomato pieces and wine, then turn up the heat and boil for a few moments. Turn the heat down and add the rabit pieces, by now nicely golden brown. Add the bay leaves and sage leaves. Cover and simmer for 45 minutes (do not skim). The rabbit will have shrunk and be very tender. Adjust the seasoning.

It is now ready to serve as a casserole. If you wish to use it as a pasta sauce, allow to cool completely, then with your hands pull the meat off the bones, shredding it as you do, and returning it to the sauce. Reheat with large knob of butter, extra seasoning, and toss with cooked pappardelle (see page 75), adding grated Parmesan.

Salmi di Faraona
Salmis of Guinea Fowl

Tuesday night at La Cacciata is nearly always a big dinner at the Belcapos' villa. The guests have been away for the day, shopping and absorbing the splendours of Umbria. On returning, there is no class. They're obviously too tired to prepare their own dinner, and so am I. Clara Belcapo and her maid Marissa cook for us, her husband pours the Prosecco, and the chambermaids double as waitresses. The dinner follows a sure and certain pattern: crostini with 'toppings'; home-made noodles with the estate oil, chilli and herbs, then often this excellent guinea fowl braised in the estate's red wine.

4 people
1 guinea fowl, approx. 1.5 kg (ask
　　your butcher to joint it and cut it
　　into 8 pieces in all)
seasoned flour

Dust the pieces of guinea fowl with the seasoned flour. Take a wide pan or casserole which will hold the meat in one layer. Heat a little oil in this over a medium heat and gently brown the guinea fowl. Be careful not to burn, as the taste of scorched flour is impossible to get rid of.

good olive oil

100 g pancetta, cut into small
lardons

200 g button mushrooms, washed
and earthy stalk bases removed

200 g button onions, peeled

1 bottle red wine, preferably
Sangiovese

4 tbsp red wine vinegar

2 bay leaves, 1 sprig each of
parsley and thyme, tied into a
bouquet garni

salt and pepper

4 Crostini (see page 102)

chicken liver topping for Crostini
(see page 102) or, much easier,
a good quality chicken pâté
(optional)

a handful of parsley leaves

When the pieces are uniformly golden brown add the pancetta and a little more oil. Continue to cook steadily until this turns translucent, then add the mushrooms and onions. Continue sautéing carefully, turning the pieces of fowl occasionally, for about 10 minutes or until the vegetables have coloured slightly. Add the vinegar and boil for 1 minute then pour in the red wine and add the bouquet garni. Return to a simmer and then turn the heat to low. The pieces of bird should be about half covered in the wine; if not, add a little water. Braise gently for an hour, turning and basting often. If the liquid level drops too much, add a little water; the final level should have reduced by approximately one-half, and be a deep red colour with a glossy sheen. Check that the bird is very tender, nearly falling off the bones; if not return it to cook for a little longer. Check the seasoning.

Serve with crostini spread with liver paste under the pieces of guinea fowl, and the mushrooms, pancetta, onions and syrupy sauce spooned on top. Scatter with a little coarsely chopped parsley. Italian Coq au Vin!

Little **Tip**

■ Leftover meat sauce with the bones removed
makes an excellent sauce for pappardelle. Simply
reheat with a large knob of butter and dress the
cooked noodles sparingly with it and Parmesan.

Tacchino Tonnato
Cold Turkey with Tuna Sauce

Oddly enough, turkey is a popular meat in Umbria, and there it is raised to have some flavour. Legs and breasts are sold separately.

You would be unwise to tell your dinner guests the English translation of this dish before they taste it. This is an Umbrian adaption of the North Italian speciality, Vitello Tonnato. This substitution crops up a lot round Orvieto; turkey breast is roasted with rosemary like veal rump, escalopes of fillet are breaded and fried like Scallopini di Vitello, the legs are braised in red wine. Anything at all except roast the whole bird: the Italians are too canny with their ingredients, clever enough to always butcher a large bird and use the different parts to their best advantage. The part of the recipe devoted to roasting the breast makes a delicious hot dish without the tuna sauce, perhaps a hot dish one day then cold the next. Sounds like Christmas?

The turkey breast should be boned, skinned and not stuffed. If you get one from the supermarket, untie it and remove the stuffing and skin, re-tie and proceed.

Lots of people!

1 x 1–2 kg turkey breast, boned, rolled and tied (see above)

salt and pepper

about 2 tbsp good olive oil

2 glasses dry white wine

1 sprig rosemary (optional)

2 small tins anchovies, drained and split lengthways

2 tbsp capers, rinsed

For the tuna sauce:

1 x 250 g tin tuna (best-quality in olive oil or drained of brine)

1 egg

a handful of parsley leaves

juice of 1 lemon

approx. 500 ml good olive oil

The morning or day before serving, roast the turkey breast. Preheat the oven to 180°C/350°F/Gas 4. Season the joint very liberally. Find a flameproof casserole into which the turkey will fit snugly. Heat the casserole with a little oil over a medium flame. Drop the meat in and brown very thoroughly on all sides, about 10 minutes. This is very important, as the major taste in the meat comes from the well browned and wine-basted exterior.

Add the wine and baste. Place uncovered in the oven for 15 minutes then reduce the temperature to 150°C/300°F/Gas 2 and continue roasting for a further 30 minutes, basting and turning frequently. If all the wine evaporates, add a little water. A sprig of rosemary is very welcome addition to this dish.

Check for doneness by inserting a small knife into the centre of the joint; leave for a few seconds then remove and test the heat of the blade on your lips. If you burn your lips the turkey is too done. If warm, then the meat is perfect; if cold or very lukewarm, return to the oven for a further 15 minutes, moistening with water as necessary.

Allow the turkey to cool, out of the fridge, occasionally rolling it over in the remaining pan juices.

To make the tuna sauce, it's food processor time! My kind of cooking: put the egg, parsley, tuna and lemon juice in the processor bowl, season and whirl.

Now add the oil in a thin stream with the machine running until you have a thick mayonnaise-like substance. Check the seasoning and acidity, and add more oil or lemon to your taste. Remove from the food processor bowl, but do not refrigerate, it may separate. Do not make too long in advance either as the fragrance of the lemon and parsley quickly fade.

To assemble the dish, cut the turkey into 1 cm steaks across the breast. Arrange one or two smaller slices on individual plates. Coat the meat with tuna sauce and arrange the painfully halved anchovies in a grid pattern on each one. (Think noughts and crosses here.) Dot each square with a caper and serve with an extra wedge of lemon if you fancy.

Little Tip

- Add 1 tbsp tomato ketchup to this sauce – quite delicious. The dish is also extremely good with a tomato salad.

Coscia di Tacchino Arrosto
Roast Turkey Leg

4 people

2 turkey legs (ask your butcher to bone them, but to give you the bones)
500 g spinach or Swiss chard, washed
good olive oil
2 garlic cloves, peeled and minced
salt and pepper
200 g pancetta, diced
1 onion, 1 carrot and 1 celery stick, all minced into a fine soffritto
1/2 bottle red wine
500 ml Chicken Broth (see page 186)

Cook the spinach in a large frying pan in a little olive oil over a very high heat until just wilted. Add the garlic and allow to cool. Squeeze out when cool, then season. Stuff the turkey legs with the spinach, and re-form into approximately their previous shape. Tie about four times.

Preheat the oven to 180°C/350°F/Gas 4.

Heat a roasting dish with a little oil and add the pancetta and the turkey bones. Cook over a medium flame until the pancetta starts to colour. Add the turkey legs and soffritto, and continue sweating for 10 minutes or so over a medium flame. At this point add the red wine and broth. Place in the roasting dish in the preheated oven and roast for an hour, turning and basting the turkey often. This is left uncovered and the sauce will reduce to a glaze. Add more water if needed.

If after an hour the turkey is done but the sauce is still thin, remove the turkey and turn the heat up and reduce on top of the stove until strongly flavoured and syrupy. Pick out and discard the bones and skim the fat off the sauce. Slice the turkey rolls across the grain and serve with the pancetta and soffritto sauce.

Pesce

Fish Until recently Italians away from the coast rarely ate seafood. They would eat baccala (salt cod) on feast days, and make good use of the abundant lake and river fish. This was as true of Rome 25 km inland, as it was of Orvieto 90 km away from the sea. Umbria is Italy's only landlocked province, and has a particularly large repertoire of freshwater fish cookery, two recipes of which are given here.

In the last twenty years, Italy's seafood cuisine has expanded from the fishing ports into the interior, taking with it the essentially simple cooking techniques of grilling, baking, deep-frying of small fish and the making of bouillabaisse-like stews. In nearly all cases fish are left intact, scaled and gutted, yes, but heads are on and bones are in. This is the best way to eat fish, and I think people who are outfaced by the beady eye of a whole fish on their plate are wimps!

At La Cacciata we have limited access to very good fish. We use salt cod; shellfish are available for pasta dishes and seafood risotto; we can get squid; and lake fishes such as eel, pike and coregone (a large fish similar to grayling) are available. With this paucity of resources in contrast to vegetables, fruit, poultry and meat, seafood does not assume a big role in the cooking of the school. However, for reference, I include general comments on grilling, baking and frying fish as well as those recipes we have successfully deployed at the school.

PESCE ALLA GRIGLIA | GRILLED FISH

When grilling whole fish, size is very important. The Italians do not attempt to grill minuscule red mullet, they deep-fry them. Nor do they cook very large bass or bream by this method, but roast or bake them instead. The ideal size range for grilling is between 300 g and 1 kg. Fish in this range can be cooked through relatively quickly, preventing dry overcooked flesh, yet are big enough to allow the skin to crisp, an important part of their appeal.

The other important component is freshness. The reason the Italians insist on being served whole fish is because they want to see it before cooking to ensure its quality. Paul Minichelli at Le Duc in Paris used to serve a dish of grilled sea bass which he merely gutted, it was not scaled or seasoned, but simply cooked under a salamander or overhead grill. The fish had to be line-caught and was unbelievably fresh, but when it came to the table, with the waiter expertly filleting it for you, it was the very essence of the sea. There was no sauce, no lemon, no oil, no garnish, just the gleaming white meat. Fantastic.

What sort of grill? Good results are very easy to achieve with a domestic overhead grill, providing the whole fish will fit under and can be at least 6 cm away from the flame. More difficult but equally delicious is cooking on a ridged cast-iron grill, and most difficult of all but indubitably the best, is over a barbecue. A useful piece of kit for barbecues are those racks that sandwich the fish allowing you to turn them without actually risking handling the things directly.

Cooking times are hard to give, and practice and judgment are necessary here. Perhaps you should practise on mackerel before you graduate to sea bass or royal sea bream. The methodology is the same, the cost of failure is not! Incidentally, very fresh grilled mackerel is one of the nicest fish to eat.

What fish to grill

In general round-bodied, slightly oily scaled fish like sea bass, various types of sea bream, mackerel, sea trout, very fresh grey mullet and the larger red mullet.

Sardines grill very well despite being out of the size parameters, as do pilchards and large fresh anchovies. Some shellfish like langoustines, small lobsters, large clams and razor shells also cook spectacularly well on a barbecue though they require care and attention.

Squid, both whole small ones or steaks cut from larger ones, are interesting and quick to grill. They benefit from marinating, and the larger pieces curl up in architectural ways despite scoring them.

What fish not to grill

I do not like char-grilled white fish. Turbot, brill, halibut and sole are too delicate in taste and texture for the inevitable scorching they receive. (The present 'grill everything' trend in cooking is simple ignorance and lack of culinary intelligence.) However, these fish can be cooked under an overhead grill very successfully. The reason being that there is no contact with hot metal or coals: the fish is cooked by convection, the action of heat and air. I have even seen the lunacy of char-grilled cod on a menu, though I suspect it was just striped on the grill then baked. Imagine trying to chisel a wet, flaking, disintegrating piece of cod off the barbecue!

Sgombro
Grilled Mackerel

This is the template recipe for grilling fish. Master this, and you'll be able to grill any fish.

4 people

4 whole mackerel, 300 g each,
    gutted by your fishmonger (ask
    him to remove the gills as well)
sea salt
lemon wedges

- Larger fish do not differ much in method, cooking times do not double because the fish is twice as big. Examination of the slashes should give you some indication of what is happening. Fins become very easy to pull out in fully cooked fish. Don't be afraid to cut deeper into one of the slashes to expose the spine and ascertain how cooked the beast is.

You will need a barbecue, ridged grill pan or overhead grill. When grilling whole fish it is important that no trace of blood remains in the body cavity as this goes a very unpleasant colour when cooked. To remove, rub with sea salt then brush out with an old toothbrush and a little water.

Cut two slashes on each side of the fish nearly down to the spine then salt the fish heavily. Grill by your chosen method for approximately 5 minutes per side. The side you present to the heat first will be the side you serve uppermost because it will have the most appetising appearance.

If using a ridged grill pan cook the fish aligned with the ridges and not across them, this makes turning easier as you can slide a long pronged cooking fork along the grooves right under the full length of the fish and simply flip it over. When you grill the fish across the ridges you need two forks, one at the head and one at the tail, and still risk the fish breaking in the middle as you turn it. Serve the fish hot with lemon wedges.

Baccala con Ceci Belcapo

Signor Belcapo's Olive-harvest Salt Cod and Chickpeas

This dish is served to all the temporary workers at the end of the olive harvest some time in November. I've never been at La Cacciata at this time, but I understand it is much harder work than the grape harvest, and the weather tends to be much more inclement. Clara Belcapo showed me how to make the dish last summer, and the only alterations I've permitted myself are to add a little broth and substitute home-salted cod for the rather overpowering stockfish authentically used. You must try and find good-quality chickpeas; the Spanish brands are by far the best. Large old chickpeas are useless, the fresher the better.

4–6 people

1 kg Home-salted Cod (see page 44),
  cut into 250 g steaks
500 g chickpeas, soaked overnight
1 chilli pepper
4 garlic cloves
2 bay leaves
1 recipe Gremolata (see page 125)
500 ml Chicken Broth (see page 186)
black pepper
top-quality olive oil (ideally the brand-
  new oil in November/December
  to go with the new season's
  chickpeas)

Put the salt cod to desalinate in a tray in the sink under a gently running tap. Drain the chickpeas, rinse thoroughly, then drain again and put in a largish pan. Add double their volume of water, and bring to the boil over a high heat. They will throw a considerable scum which, if allowed to boil back into the cooking liquid, will heighten the chickpeas' already flatulent reputation. Skim this off, and turn the heat to low so the peas are simmering. Split the chilli lengthways and add with the whole unpeeled garlic cloves and the bay leaves to the chickpeas. Simmer until very tender (al dente chickpeas are not a good idea: I once served them in this dish to A.A. Gill, the *Sunday Times'* restaurant critic, he wasn't impressed), and leave to cool in their liquor. You may need to skim from time to time during cooking. The peas may take as little as an hour but will more likely be nearer 2 hours.

To serve, prepare the gremolata, then drain the cod and pat dry. Heat the chicken broth, then add an equal amount of the pea liquor. Heat 8 heaped serving spoons of peas in this liquor. Warm the soup plates in a low oven.

The cod is quickly cooked in a non-stick frying pan. If you haven't got one big enough to hold the fish comfortably, you will need to do it in two batches. Season the cod copiously with coarsely grated black pepper but no salt. Over a high heat fry the cod, skin side down, in a little oil for 5 minutes. Carefully turn and cook for 3 minutes on the other side. While the cod is cooking, ladle the peas and broth into warm soup plates then put the cooked cod on top. Scatter with gremolata and finally lots and lots of the olive oil.

Tonno al Forno
Baked Tuna

For this dish you need boneless tuna loin, not a steak, which must be very fresh and showing a good rosy to red colour, not a deep meat colour with a metallic sheen. The leftovers are very good for Tacchino Tonnato or Tonno e Fagioli (see pages 144 and 49).

6 people

1.25 kg loin of tuna, from back
    or belly
6 anchovy fillets
1 sprig fresh mint
2 garlic cloves, peeled
good olive oil
salt and pepper
250 g tinned tomato pieces
1 red onion, peeled and sliced
juice of 1 lemon
400 ml dry white wine
2 sprigs fresh rosemary
1 chicken stock cube (optional)

Little **Tip**

■ **If you wish to serve this dish cold
(it's delicious with potato salad),
then reduce the cooking time by 10
minutes but allow the tuna to cool in
its juices, neglecting to add the
extra wine, water and stock cube.**

Preheat the oven to 180°C/350°F/Gas 4.

Skin the tuna and cut away the dark bloody bits. Rinse and dry. Chop the anchovy, mint and garlic finely, then mix them together. With the point of a knife make incisions in the tuna 6 cm apart and 3 cm deep; fill these incisions with the chopped mix.

Rub olive oil, salt and pepper over the tuna, and put in a roasting dish that is just big enough to hold it with the tinned tomato pieces and their juice. Scatter the red onion over and about it, and put in the oven with possibly a little more oil on top. Brown in the oven for 10 minutes, then turn and add the lemon juice and 200 ml of the wine. Brown for a further 10 minutes in the oven, then baste and lower the heat to 140°C/275°F/Gas 1. Cook for 30 minutes longer, basting occasionally. When the cooking time has elapsed, remove the tuna carefully from the roasting dish and transfer to a serving dish.

Add 200 ml water, the rosemary and the remaining wine to the by now abundant juices. Reduce these over a high heat with the onions until there is just enough liquid to coat the onions. Add the stock cube if you wish. (The Italians call stock cubes *dado* for some reason.)

Serve the tuna warm with roast cubed potatoes. Spoon the onions and juice over.

Dentice Arrosto con Patate
Roast Sea Bream with Potatoes

The fish to use for this recipe is royal sea bream. These are identified by the bass-like silvery grey colour, rather imperial Roman bump on their nose, and their astronomical cost. Other bream like red or black, or red mullet, are less good, but if fresh, perfectly acceptable. The fish is baked on a bed of sliced potatoes and onions, moistened with olive oil. I first ate this fish in a transport café near Livorno; would that the British greasy spoons could even come close.

It's preferable to use one fish, but two smaller ones would do. Sea bass can be substituted successfully. Ask your fishmonger to scale, de-gill and gut the fish. See page 149 for how to clean the interior.

4–6 people
1 x 1.5 kg royal sea bream (see bank
    manager for second mortgage!)
good olive oil
4 large potatoes, peeled, thinly
    sliced, then rinsed
1 large onion, peeled and sliced
    into rings
2 garlic cloves, peeled and minced
a handful of parsley, chopped
salt and pepper
2 lemons

Preheat the oven to 180°C/350°F/Gas 4. You will need a heavy roasting tray that can comfortably house the fish. Oil this lightly. Drain and dry the potatoes and mix them in a bowl with the onions, garlic and parsley. Add 4 tbsp of olive oil, season and toss. Arrange in the roasting dish and press down. Put the roasting dish in the oven for 20 minutes to give the potatoes a head start before you add the fish.

Lightly oil the fish and cut two slashes in each side nearly through to the spine. Put a few slices of lemon in the interior of each fish and season there as well. Place the fish, staring beadily at you, on the potatoes, moisten with olive oil and season, then roast for 20 minutes.

Remove from the oven and check for doneness, it may well need 5–10 minutes more. The easiest way to check for doneness is to insert a small knife near the dorsal line on the top side of the fish and prize apart the flesh until you can see the backbone; if the flesh is still pink and adhering tenaciously to the bone, put back in the oven, having moistened it with a little more olive oil. If the skin of the fish has not browned and crisped then flash under your overhead grill for a minute or so. The bottom side of the fish will have cooked more quickly due to its contact with the potatoes but will remain moist due to trapped steam.

Serve in the roasting dish and dissect it yourself for your guests, serving the potatoes alongside. Lemon wedges are essential, as is, perhaps, a little top-quality oil to drizzle on the fish.

Anguilla allo Spiedo
Roast Eels with Pancetta and Bay Leaves

Lago di Trasimeno is Umbria's largest lake, and this dish of fat eel steaks, wrapped in thin pancetta and skewered with bay leaves and roasted over a wood fire, is the best of the local fish specialities. If you like eels, then this has to be one of the best dishes in the world; if you don't like eels, you haven't even read this far. I have opted to cook this in a hot oven rather than on a barbecue because this seems more achievable.

A large eel is better for this dish than two small ones. The tail section and head can be discarded, leaving you with 500–600 g, approximately three steaks per person.

4 people
800 g eel, skinned and cut into
    12 x 3 cm steaks
12 thin slices smoked pancetta (or
    streaky bacon)
8 bay leaves, fresh if possible
salt and coarse black pepper
good olive oil

Preheat the oven to its maximum. Soak 4 wooden skewers in water for an hour.

Wrap each eel steak in the pancetta around the dark blue membrane, then pin the pancetta with a skewer. Add a bay leaf, then another piece of wrapped eel. There should be 3 eel steaks and 2 bay leaves on each skewer. Salt lightly and more generously scatter with coarse black pepper.

Prepare a roasting tray with a rack in it. Lay the eel kebabs on this and roast for 25 minutes. It is important that the skewers are not too tightly packed as this inhibits the cooking; the pieces should be barely touching. You may if you wish brush the eels with olive oil halfway through cooking, but the eels are so fatty this is not necessary. If the bay leaves and pancetta start to scorch before the cooking time has elapsed, turn the oven down to 180°C/350°F/Gas 4 and loosely cover the kebabs with aluminium foil.

Serve with plain boiled potatoes which have been scattered with chopped parsley and butter.

Tortino d'Alici e Patate
Anchovy and Potato Tart

This is a dish we often serve to the guests as a nibble on arrival. It comes originally from Puglia (the heel of Italy) and can only be made with fresh anchovies, not tinned or jarred. Small fresh sardines or herrings make an acceptable substitute. Boning anchovies sounds micro-surgical, but is in fact simplicity itself.

1 tart for 4 people as an appetiser
   or lunch dish
500 g potatoes (not new, regular
   'bakers' are fine), peeled
500 g large fresh anchovies
salt and pepper
2 tbsp good olive oil
1/2 tsp oregano (dried is fine)
2 garlic cloves, peeled and minced
200 g Crisp Breadcrumbs (see
   page 189)
2 tsp chopped parsley

Preheat the oven to 180°C/350°F/Gas 4. You will need a non-stick ovenproof frying pan 25 cm in diameter.

Slice the potatoes very thinly and keep in cold water until needed. Now for the anchovies. Rinse them lightly and then cut or pull off the heads and discard. With your thumb and forefinger, run down either side of the spine, pressing gently. The fillets will start to come away. As this happens, open up the fish and pull the bones out. You will now have two fillets joined at the belly in a triangular shape. Rinse carefully, especially in the belly area, and lay out on a tray. Season lightly and add a little oil. Refrigerate.

Drain the potatoes and pat dry. Lightly oil the frying pan and arrange the slices in overlapping circles to form a potato galette. Sprinkle with more oil, the oregano and a little chopped garlic, and season lightly. Put the pan over a medium heat and cook until the potatoes start to fry in the oil: do not stir or shake. Put the pan in the oven for 10 minutes to part-cook the potatoes. Remove from the oven and allow to cool a little.

Mix the breadcrumbs with the remaining garlic and the parsley, and process to a fine meal. Arrange the anchovy fillets in a radial pattern on the potato galette. Scatter with breadcrumbs to coat lightly, moisten with a little oil and return to the oven for 10 minutes to cook the anchovies.

The tart can be assembled and held until needed but the final baking must be at the last minute. As soon as the tart is ready, slide a flexible spatula under the edges of the potato base to check that it hasn't stuck. Then carefully but swiftly tilt the tart out of the pan and on to a chopping board. (This is why you needed a non-stick pan.) Cut into wedges – a pizza cutter is best for this – and eat immediately.

Insalata di Luccio
Pike Salad

This is one of the only sane ways of treating pike. Dishes like Quenelles de Brochet require pushing the pulped fish flesh through a fine sieve to remove innumerable bones, a job only to be wished on the disciples of Marco Pierre White or other three-Michelin-starred chefs. Here the fish is poached, allowed to cool in its poaching liquid, then flaked carefully by hand, a much easier method of de-boning. Your fishmonger will be able to get pike if you push him.

The weight quoted here is a cleaned weight, i.e. no head, guts or tail. A 1.5 kg fish will be fine if you have pike-fishing friends. (You can substitute large mackerel successfully.)

6 people

1 x 1 kg pike
1/2 bottle dry white wine
2 large onions, peeled and cut
    into rings
4 medium carrots, cut into
    matchsticks
1 celery heart, green outer leaves
    removed, sliced into rings
2 bay leaves, but Kaffir lime leaves
    would be better
1 wine glass white wine vinegar
salt and pepper
1 bunch parsley
12 black peppercorns
very good olive oil

The day before cut the fish into 5 cm thick steaks (have your fishmonger do this for you), and leave in cold salted water overnight. This will remove the second drawback to pike, its slightly muddy taste.

Put the wine, vegetables, bay leaves and vinegar in a wide casserole. Add 1.5 litres water, season with a generous amount of salt, and add the parsley stalks and peppercorns. Bring this mixture to the boil, turn down the heat and simmer for 30 minutes. Then add the pike steaks, return to the boil, cover and turn off the heat. Allow the fish to cool nearly completely in this court-bouillon.

Pick out the pike, peel off the skin and, working patiently, pull the cooked flesh away from the bones, placing it in a bowl. Drain the court-bouillon, reserving 200 ml of liquid and all the vegetables. Discard the bay leaves, peppercorns and parsley stalks. Mix the vegetables with the pike flesh (they will be crunchy and slightly pickled from the court-bouillon whose acidity prevents them from softening). Refrigerate the bowl.

Put the reserved court-bouillon on to boil and reduce by at least 70 per cent. Taste for excess salt and acidity, remembering that it is a dressing base, so it should be strongly flavoured. Add 350 ml olive oil and return to the boil, then remove from the heat immediately and whisk thoroughly to cool and emulsify. When cool, add to the pike and vegetables, and toss thoroughly. Chop the parsley leaves coarsely and add to the salad, tossing again. Do not refrigerate the salad once dressed.

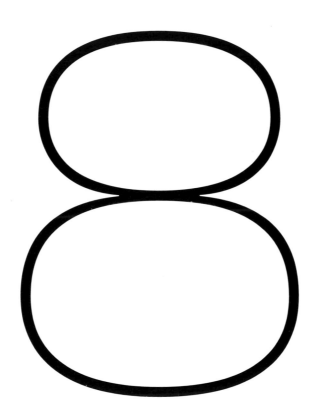

Contorni

Vegetables The Italians have a wholly different attitude to the serving of vegetables than the British. They see no need to accompany their main courses with a large selection of other inappropriate vegetables. They will usually serve one vegetable dish at the same time as the main course, plus possibly some potatoes.

The differences between vegetable contorni and vegetable antipasti are often blurred. Many of the dishes listed at the beginning of the book make suitable accompaniments.

Puree di Patate
Mashed Potato

What I basically recommend is that you use your own recipe for mashed potato here. I personally favour one made with a little milk, a lot of butter and a little optional double cream. However, at various points in the book we recommend rather more obscure mashed potatoes. These can either be made with olive oil or butter, but *not both*.

Olive Mash
Make your mashed potatoes as you always do, but instead of whisking in the butter, whisk in generous top-quality olive oil. Serve immediately, and do not try to reheat.

Garlic Mash
When boiling the potatoes, put a whole blanched head of garlic to cook with them. Before you make the mash, run the garlic under cold water, peel as many cloves as you think you need, and purée with the potatoes. Incidentally, boiled garlic cloves are easy to peel; you simply squeeze the pulpy flesh out of the skins. Blanch the garlic first by boiling in copious water for 10 minutes. Discard the water.

Parsley Mash
Make with either butter or olive oil, and incorporate 1 heaped tbsp chopped parsley per person.

Rocket Mash
Make the mashed potato with either butter or olive oil as above. De-stalk the rocket and chop coarsely. You will need 1 heaped tbsp per person, and this should be incorporated into the mash.

Patate Arroste con Aglio, Aceto e Rosmarino
Roast Potatoes with Vinegar, Garlic and Rosemary

Badly roasted potatoes – lukewarm, greasy and soggy – are a universal accompaniment to roast or grilled meats in most of the restaurants around Orvieto. This is my tidying up of the local speciality, and I first served it in this precise form to Signor Belcapo at the La Cacciata 'end-of-week' dinner. He went mental about them, and his wife Clara and cook Marisa now have to try and cook them the English way – as if any dish involving so many cloves of garlic could ever be seen as English...

4–6 people

8 large new potatoes, either peeled
    or scrubbed until almost totally
    skinless
good olive oil
salt and pepper
24 garlic cloves, new season and
    left in their skins
1 sprig rosemary
2–3 tbsp good ordinary red wine
    vinegar

- Get your timing right on this dish.
  If you can bring the potatoes out
  of the oven at exactly the right time
  to accompany your main course,
  they will be incomparable, but they
  do not hold for long.

Preheat the oven to its maximum.

Cut the potatoes into large bite-sized pieces. Cover with cold water in a pan and bring to a boil, switch off and leave for 10 minutes. Drain well.

Grease a roasting dish that is big enough to hold the potatoes in a single layer liberally with olive oil, then arrange the potatoes in it with a flat cut surface in contact with the dish. Sprinkle with more olive oil and season liberally with coarse salt and pepper. Roast in the oven for 30 minutes until brown and crisp. (This may take more than 30 minutes.)

Turn to another face and strew the potatoes with the garlic cloves. Turn the oven down to 160°C/325°F/Gas 3 and give them a further 15 minutes. You may need a little more olive oil. After this time is up, strew with the rosemary needles and turn the garlic and potatoes again. Return to the oven and give a further 15 minutes. Test for doneness and seasoning. Remove from the oven and sprinkle with the vinegar, shake the dish and stand back; it will splutter. Serve immediately.

Costellette di Patate al Forno
Oven Chips

The simplest of roast potato dishes, this one is particularly delicious with the potatoes available at La Cacciata throughout the summer. Similar types available in Britain are Cyprus, large news, Egyptian large or new King Edwards.

4–6 people

6 large new potatoes, well scrubbed
100 ml good olive oil, or the
    equivalent amount of home-
    rendered lard, beef dripping or
    goose fat
salt and pepper
red wine vinegar

Preheat the oven to 180°C/350°F/Gas 4.

Put the oil or fat into the roasting dish, it should be about 1 cm deep. Slice the potatoes into 2 cm thick rounds. For the moment ignore the smaller rounded end pieces, and arrange the larger central slices tightly in the roasting dish; fill the gaps with the ends. Season and bake in the oven for 30 minutes. Very carefully remove from the oven and lift one potato from the centre to see if it is golden brown. If so, turn all the potatoes and return to the oven until tender, probably about 15 minutes. By this time most of the oil or fat will be absorbed and hopefully not too many of the potatoes will have stuck. Chisel them out carefully and arrange on a hot serving plate. Sprinkle with a little vinegar and sea salt.

Cipolline in Agrodolce
Sweet and Sour Onions

Pickling onions peeled (be prepared for some tears) and cooked with vinegar, sugar, pine nuts, butter and corinth raisins. Another Venetian dish clearly demonstrating that city's link with the Middle East. This can be served as an antipasto or as a contorno.

4–6 people
800 g large pickling onions, peeled
55 g butter
1 1/2 tbsp sugar
65 ml red wine vinegar
30 g corinth raisins (if you can get
  them, otherwise Whitworths)
35 g pine nuts
salt and pepper

■ At La Cacciata this dish is
  often made with olive oil instead of
  butter, and served at room
  temperature as an antipasto.

Trim the top and bottom of the onions minimally, otherwise they will break up during cooking.

Set the oven to low, 140°C/275°F/Gas 1.

Take a pan wide enough to hold the onions in a single layer and melt the butter in this over a medium flame. As soon as this starts to brown, add the sugar and half the vinegar. Add the onions and stir to coat. Cook over a low flame uncovered, but not stirring, for about 20 minutes. The onions will render a little liquid which will combine with the butter, vinegar and sugar. This liquid should be reduced by half during this process. Turn the onions carefully once during this time. Now add the raisins, pine nuts and the remaining vinegar. Mix carefully and bake in the oven for 45 minutes, turning occasionally, until caramel-brown.

This dish is best served warm. If you try to serve it hot, the sugar content may scald your guests' palates.

Schiafata
Braised Broad Beans with Pancetta and Swiss Chard

This is one of Clara Belcapo's recipes, normally served as a dish in its own right.

6–8 people
300 g broad beans, approx. 1.3 kg
  before podding
5 tbsp good olive oil
100 g streaky pancetta, finely diced
1 carrot, 1 onion and 2 celery sticks,
  very finely diced for a soffritto
2 garlic cloves, peeled and minced
1 glass white wine
150 g tinned tomato pieces
1.5 kg Swiss chard, prepared
  (see page 18)
salt and pepper

In a medium to large casserole heat the oil over a medium flame. Add the pancetta and sweat for 5 minutes, then add the soffritto and garlic and sweat for a further 5 minutes. Now add the beans and continue sweating together for yet another 5 minutes. Add the wine, the tomato pieces and their juices and stir. Cover and simmer for half an hour, then add the Swiss chard which you should have coarsely chopped. Stir, taste, adust the seasoning, cover and continue to simmer for a further half hour. This may seem an excessive time to cook fresh broad beans and chard, but it takes that long for all the flavours, particularly the tomato, to blend to a harmonious whole – honest!

Fagioli di Toscana
Braised Haricot Beans with Pancetta

A wonderful baked bean dish. The simple action of assembling the dish and then baking the beans in the oven seems to dramatically alter their taste and texture. This dish cannot be successfully done on top of the cooker.

8 people

500 g haricot beans, soaked
    overnight and rinsed thoroughly
6 garlic cloves in their skins
1 large red chilli pepper
2 bay leaves
200 g smoked pancetta in the
    piece, trimmed and cut into
    lardons
good olive oil
1 carrot, peeled and cut into
    1 cm dice
2 celery sticks, peeled and cut into
    1 cm dice
1 onion, peeled and cut into
    1 cm dice
500 g tinned tomato pieces with
    their juices

Little **Tip**

- With extra bean cooking liquid added (enough to cover the beans by 3 cm), you have an excellent base for cassoulet here. Simply add duck confit, a good sausage sliced up (cotechino), and some sautéed lamb pieces.

Cover the soaked beans with fresh cold water and bring to the boil. Skim, and add the garlic, chilli and bay leaves and simmer for about 1 hour or until nearly tender.

Preheat the oven to 180°C/350°F/Gas 4.

While the beans are cooking prepare the rest of the ingredients, starting with the pancetta. Heat a little olive oil in a casserole big enough to hold the vegetables, pancetta and beans comfortably. Add the pancetta and cook over a medium heat, stirring occasionally, until it has coloured and rendered a lot of fat, about 10–15 minutes. Add the carrot, celery and onion, and sweat for a further 5 minutes until glistening and coated in the pancetta fat. Add the tomato pieces and their juices and bring to a simmer.

Check if the beans are nearly tender, then transfer them to the casserole with a slotted spoon or spider. (Do not throw away their liquor.) Pick out the chilli and garlic, chop them (after discarding the garlic skins), then add to the casserole. Stir all this together then add enough of the bean cooking liquor to just cover everything. Stir again. Cover the casserole and bake for 1 hour.

Remove from the oven and set aside for 15 minutes to allow the casserole to reduce to sub-volcanic temperatures. Remove the lid at the table. The beans should not need seasoning, the pancetta and chilli will have seen to that.

Sautéed Spinach or Swiss Chard

Prepare the greens as for Insalata di Bietole (see page 18). When you need to use them, merely sauté gently in a frying pan with a little olive oil, salt and pepper. Serve with a lemon wedge.

Cavolo Rosso

Red Cabbage

Not an immediate choice when Italian vegetable cooking springs to mind, however certain principles used are very Italian, especially the sweet and sour 'gastric' made before the cabbage is started. This dish is virtually inseparable from the Roast Belly of Pork on page 134; it takes roughly the same amount of time and attention, and is cooked in the same oven. Together they make a hearty and simple winter dinner. Like the pork, the cabbage is good cold or reheated.

This may not be fast food, but it is simple food. You will need a cast-iron casserole with a lid, and a food processor with a slicer blade would be helpful for the cabbage.

8 people

1 red cabbage, about 1.5 kg,
     finely sliced
4 juniper berries
10 black peppercorns
sea salt and pepper
a little sunflower oil
1 large onion, peeled and sliced
2 bay leaves
1 large sprig rosemary
2 tbsp caster sugar
2 tbsp red wine vinegar

Preheat the oven to 180°C/350°F/Gas 4.

In a small pan toast the juniper berries for 3–4 minutes with the peppercorns, then add 1/2 tbsp sea salt and transfer to a pestle and mortar or spice grinder, and pulverise. Heat 2 tbsp sunflower oil in the casserole over a high heat, then add the onion and colour lightly. Add the juniper berry mix to the onion, then the bay leaves and rosemary leaves stripped from the sprig. The onion should now be browning. Toss and add the sugar, then continue cooking for a minute or so to allow the sugar to caramelise slightly. Add the vinegar and continue cooking over a high heat until the vinegar has evaporated. Add the cabbage and, off the heat, mix thoroughly. Cover and put in the oven with the pork. After half an hour remove both dishes: stir the cabbage and carefully pour any fat accumulating in the pork roasting pan over the cabbage. Cover the cabbage again, and return both dishes to the oven.

If you insist on ignoring my advice and cooking the cabbage on its own, then add copious quantities of dripping or duck fat instead of sunflower oil at the beginning of the cooking procedure. Ideally you should repeat the procedure of moistening the cabbage with the fat one more time. The cabbage should go into the oven after the pork, when the temperature is turned down to 180°C/350°F/Gas 4.

When you serve it, try to find and discard the bay leaves. Serve the cabbage in a mound under the roast belly pork.

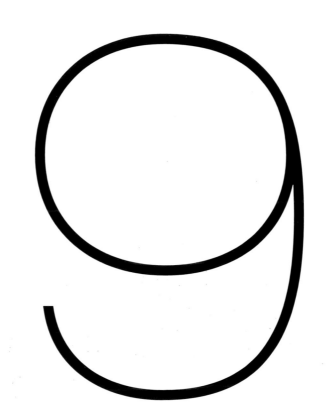

Dolci

Desserts We have been told that there is no great scope for dessert in an Italian meal. Pastries and cakes are normally taken with coffee as a snack, and meals traditionally end with cheese and fruit. This accepted wisdom is questionable. Certainly large quantities of pastries are consumed in Italy's innumerable coffee bars, but recent experience has shown that Italians often opt to finish their meal with a dessert. The rise and rise of tiramisù!

CROSTATE DI FRUTTA | FRUIT TARTS

La Cacciata has several cherry trees, at least two fig trees, and peaches, apples, pears and quinces all available for making desserts in their appropriate seasons. With this abundance on hand, it's hardly surprising that fruit tarts have become in a way the definitive dessert throughout the season out there.

You will need a frozen pastry shell (see below) and the almond frangipane mix (opposite), otherwise the method is very simple. Be careful to fully cook these pastries, for what may appear to be fully cooked judging by the top may well have raw frangipane and a soggy bottom of pastry (never desirable in tarts). The raw pastry shell is taken straight from the freezer and filled to a depth of 1 cm only with the frangipane mixture, then the prepared fruit is pushed into the mix but still protruding. The tart then goes in a 180°C/350°F/Gas 4 oven for 30 minutes, during which time the frangipane will rise and nearly engulf the fruit and everything will start to brown. At this point the oven is turned down to 150°C/300°F/Gas 2 and the tart continues baking and drying out for a further 45 minutes. The best indicator that everything's completely cooked is the edges of the tart detaching themselves from the pastry case as they shrink when cooked. A clean knife inserted into the frangipane near the tart's centre should also come out clean.

I prefer to prepare these pastries some time in advance, often in the morning, for service at dinner. This in effect means that you have one course all present and correct before you start the main bulk of the cooking. This can induce a strong sense of well-being as your plans for a dinner party proceed.

Pastry Shell

The quantities given make three tart or crostata shells.

150 g caster sugar
100 g ground almonds
500 g plain flour
500 g butter, cut into small dice
1 whole egg
2 egg yolks
1/2 tsp grated lemon zest
1 tsp rum
a pinch of salt

You will need three 20–25 cm loose-bottomed flan tins and one or two baking sheets.

Put the sugar, almonds and flour into a food processor and turn on at full speed for a few seconds. Add the butter dice and work again until just blended in. The mixture will resemble fine breadcrumbs. Add the egg and yolks, the lemon zest, rum and a minute pinch of salt, and work again until the pastry forms into a ball.

Scrape this out on to a sheet of clingfilm and roll up the film to form the dough into a cylinder with a diameter of 5 cm. Chill for at least 2 hours.

The dough is impossible to roll out, so cut thin discs off the end of the cylinder and overlap them slightly to cover the bottom and sides of each tart tin, pushing down with your fingers to make as even a pastry shell as possible. It should be slightly more solid round the edges and pushed right up to the top as it will shrink slightly as it bakes. Be careful to press into the corners so there is no air between the tin and the pastry.

An alternative method of rolling out the dough is to do it between two sheets of clingfilm, peeling one layer off before you lift it into the flan ring and the second when you have pressed the pastry into the ring.

Cover with clingfilm, pressing this well into the pastry case, and freeze until needed.

Blind Baking

One of the most tedious techniques in cooking is the blind baking of pastry shells, involving sheets of greaseproof paper or foil and dried beans. The beans are to hold the pastry in place, preventing it collapsing down the sides of the tart tin, and in theory giving you a partially or fully baked case ready to receive a liquid filling. In fact, two things generally happen: the pastry collapses down the sides anyway, and when you attempt to remove the foil and beans, a large section of the pastry is usually attached to it!

The pastry recipe detailed here is so short that, when baked directly from the freezer at 180°C/350°F/Gas 4, without any beans, it will form a near perfect shell. I must stress that the pastry must go into the oven hard frozen; it must not defrost for even a minute. Make sure your oven is well preheated too. My success rate on this is over 90 per cent, but even if you follow the instructions to the letter and you still have a problem, you have two more pastry shells sitting in the freezer to try.

Frangipane

This is the simplest and most robust of all the various almond mixes known collectively as frangipane. This quantity will make enough for the three tart cases in the Pastry Shell recipe. It freezes well, but will also hold for several days in the fridge.

100 g blanched almonds (these achieve a much better result than pre-ground almonds, which often tend to be rather stale)
100 g plain flour
100 g caster sugar
100 g unsalted butter
4 medium eggs

In a food processor, chop the almonds until they form a fine meal. Add the flour, sugar and the butter cut into small pieces. Process until it resembles fine crumbs. Add the eggs, and process for a minute or so until a creamy mixture is made. Scrape out of the processor into a bowl. Wrap in clingfilm and store in the fridge. You will need to take it out of the fridge an hour before needed.

CROSTATA DI ALBICOCCHE
Apricot Tart

Choose ripe apricots – for me this is the best of the myriad fruit tarts served at La Cacciata. Good-quality dried apricots plumped in a little sweetened warm water then soused with a little brandy make a very acceptable substitute.

This apricot tart represents the master recipe. I detail the various preparations needed to substitute other fruits hereafter.

6–8 people

1 Pastry Shell (see overleaf), frozen

1 recipe Frangipane (see overleaf)

1 kg ripe apricots

4 tbsp caster sugar

50 g flaked almonds

icing sugar to dust

Cut the apricots in half along their rather anatomical seam, twist and separate, then dig out the stone. Lay them in a tray and sprinkle with the sugar, massage them a little and leave to macerate for an hour.

Preheat the oven to 180°C/350°F/Gas 4. Place the frangipane mix in the still frozen pastry shell, then drain the apricots and insert them: stack them on their sides, standing almost vertically, so that they prop each other up. They shrink rather a lot during cooking so use plenty and pack the case tightly, pressing them into the frangipane.

Bake for a half an hour, then scatter with flaked almonds, and dust generously with icing sugar. Return to the oven turned down to 150°C/300°F/Gas 2 for 45 minutes more.

If the tart is getting excessively brown but is not yet fully cooked in the interior, loosely cover with foil and proceed as before.

It is not a good idea to eat the tart hot, as the fruit has a high sugar content and gets very hot. This pastry is best served warm or at room temperature. Never, never let it near a fridge.

Little **Tip**

- Under no circumstances should you fill the pastry case with frangipane to a depth greater than 1 cm. It rises like mad, will take forever to cook, and will generally upset the overall balance between fruit and other ingredients.

CILIEGE | CHERRIES

These need to be stoned if you don't want your guests suing you over damaged expensive bridgework. Macerate them like the apricots for 1 hour (a little Kirsch might be nice), then simply push them into the frangipane and bake. Use 1 kg approximately per tart, but buy more as some will be scoffed during preparation.

PRUGNE SECCHE | PRUNES

The winter version of plum tart. Soak the prunes in sweetened tea until plump. Remove stones if not already done for you and push into the frangipane. Bake as above.

MELE | APPLES

These need to be slightly precooked. Peel, core and cut the apples into 6–8 segments. Melt a little butter in a big frying pan and over a high heat sauté the apples until golden brown. A rather fun and flash thing to do here is to sprinkle a little caster sugar and whisky over them and caramelise.
Allow to cool and proceed as per the master recipe bearing in mind that the apples will shrink more, so pack in plenty.

PERE | PEARS

As for apples, but rub the segments with a little lemon before sautéing.

MELE COTOGNE | QUINCES

Choose large quinces and prepare as for apples and pears, but sauté a little longer with more sugar. Extend the cooking time by at least half an hour at 150°C/300°F/Gas 2. The quinces will take far longer than anything else to cook.

PESCHE NOCI E PESCHE | NECTARINES AND PEACHES

Exactly the same as apricots. Look out for the late season (September), red-fleshed vineyard peaches.

UVA | GRAPES

There are plenty of these at La Cacciata, but I can categorically state that they do not work in tarts like this.

PRUGNE | PLUMS

Fill a pastry shell with 2 recipes Frangipane. Cook as for the other tarts, remembering to scatter liberally with almonds and icing sugar halfway through. Meanwhile, make the recipe for Baked Plums (see page 180). Serve a slice of tart, a spoonful of the baked plums, and whipped cream or ice cream.

Little Tips

■ **This tart does not work with strawberries – what a horrible idea, cooked strawberries. It does, however, work with raspberries and brambles. A slightly different method of cooking is used (see opposite). Whisky is an undetectable substitution in any recipe that calls for Calvados.**

Torta di Lamponi e Mandorle
Raspberry and Almond Tart

Different from the other fruit tarts in the book in that the raspberries go below the frangipane mixture. A Mediterranean Bakewell tart.

6–8 people
1 Pastry Shell (see page 168), frozen
1 kg frozen raspberries (these work
    better than fresh)
caster sugar
1 recipe Frangipane (see page 169)
flaked almonds
icing sugar

Preheat the oven to 180°C/350°F/Gas 4.

Sprinkle the raspberries with caster sugar and leave in a colander to sweeten and drain at the same time. Place the drained raspberries in a single, tightly packed layer in the base of the tart shell. Very carefully put splodges of the frangipane over this – do not press it down. Do not cover completely, the splodges will melt and join up over the fruit.

Bake on a baking sheet until lightly brown and risen, about 30 minutes. Cover with flaked almonds and icing sugar. Turn the oven down to 150°C/300°F/Gas 2 and bake for a further 45 minutes.

Crostata di Formaggio di Capra e Limone
Goat's Cheese and Lemon Tart

Goat's cheese was virtually unknown in Italy until recently. Any fresh mild goat's cheese will do; hardened acerbic and dry mature cheeses will not. Feta will not do either, it is too salty.

6–8 people
1 Pastry Shell (see page 168), frozen
450 g fresh mild goat's cheese
4 eggs, beaten
170 g caster sugar
juice and grated rind of 4 lemons
600 ml double cream

Preheat the oven to 190°C/375°F/Gas 5, and blind-bake the case from frozen until fully cooked (see page 169), turning the oven down to 150°C/300°F/Gas 2.

Meanwhile, purée the goat's cheese. Add the eggs, sugar, lemon juice and some of the lemon zest, and beat. Finally add the cream and stir.

When the pastry is ready, pull the oven shelf out. Carefully pour the cheese mixture into the pastry case. Even more carefully, slide the oven shelf back into the oven to avoid the mixture slopping over if possible. In the oven at 150°C/300°F/Gas 2, bake until just set. It should still wobble. This should take about 35–40 minutes, and it should not soufflé. If it browns or swells, open the oven door for 2 minutes to reduce the temperature, and then turn down to 120°C/250°F/Gas 1/2. It is best served at room temperature with a fresh raspberry sauce.

Crostata di Ricotta e Limone
Ricotta and Lemon Tart

Very similar to the Goat's Cheese Tart, but milder in taste and more Italian. The quality of the ricotta is important. It is delicious with fresh raspberries.

6–8 people
1 Pastry Shell (see page 168), frozen
4 eggs
100 g caster sugar
350 g fresh ricotta cheese
500 ml double cream
4 large lemons

Preheat the oven to 190°C/375°F/Gas 5. Blind-bake the pastry case from frozen, turning the oven down immediately to 150°C/300°F/Gas 2. Bake for about 15 minutes until the pastry is light brown and firm.

Meanwhile, in a food processor, place the eggs, sugar, cheese and cream. Zest the lemons into this mix, then juice them, and whizz. Taste the mixture – it may need more lemon or sugar depending on taste.

When the pastry is ready, pull out the oven shelf. Very carefully fill the pastry shell with the lemon-ricotta mixture, and gingerly push the shelf and tart back into the oven, trying not to slosh it over the sides. Bake at 150°C/300°F/Gas 2 for about 20–25 minutes or until just set. Inspect after 10 minutes to see if it is rising – this should not happen! If it is rising, turn the temperature down and leave the oven door open for a minute or two which will reduce the temperature rapidly. The tart is done when it is set but still slightly wobbly.

Dolce di Panettone e Burro
Panettone Bread and Butter Pudding

As far as I know this has never been an Italian dish; instead it seems to have been invented simultaneously by various cooks around the world, not least by my colleague Richard Whittington. You will need an ovenproof dish with 5 cm high edges. Porcelain or enamelled cast-iron is best.

6–8 people
1/2–1/3 of 1 Panettone (see opposite)
100 g unsalted butter
500 ml double cream
170 g caster sugar
500 ml milk
4 eggs
2 tbsp raisins soaked in grappa (several days before)

Cut the panettone in half and then slice into 1 cm slabs. Butter these and butter the ovenproof dish. Mix the cream, sugar, milk and eggs thoroughly to a custard. Scatter the base of the dish with a few raisins then arrange the slabs of buttered panettone on top, overlapping like roof tiles. If you have not got enough slices from a 1/2 panettone to fill the dish, cut and butter some more. (Hence the rather vague quantity given above.) When the dish is covered by the layers of overlapping slices, stop and insert more raisins. Pour over all the custard mix, and poke about a bit until you are sure the liquid has penetrated under the slices.

Leave to soak for 1 hour. The panettone will by this time have absorbed some of the liquid.

Preheat the oven to 150°C/300°F/Gas 2. Find a larger dish into which your prepared pudding will fit, and put it in. Place in the oven and then half fill the outer dish or bain-marie with water. Bake for 35 minutes or so until firm but pliant to the touch. The top should be brown and slightly crusty.

This is best served at room temperature, 1–2 hours out of the oven. I have been known to scatter the top with icing sugar and brown further under the grill.

Panettone
Italian Christmas Cake

This was my assistant Steve's response to the unavailability of this speciality in summer. He laboriously translated it from an American recipe without the benefit of a set of measures.

Makes 1 loaf
12.5 g fresh yeast (6 g dried)
80 ml water plus 2 tbsp
100 g caster sugar plus 1/2 tsp
12 egg yolks
150 g butter, melted
1/2 tsp salt
500 g plain flour
grated zest of 2 lemons and 2
    oranges
100 g sultanas, soaked overnight
    in a little grappa
1 egg yolk, beaten

Dissolve the yeast in the 2 tbsp warm water with the 1/2 tsp sugar. Put the egg yolks, the remaining water and the yeast mixture into the bowl of a mixer and combine. Add the remaining sugar, the butter, salt and half of the flour, and work to a paste. Add the rest of the flour and work until it forms a ball. Turn the dough out of the machine and work by hand, adding more flour if necessary, until the texture is smooth and elastic.

Put the dough into a floured bowl, cover, and leave to rise for several hours until doubled in volume. Line a 30 cm spring-clip cake tin with a column of baking paper to increase its height by 3–4 cm.

Punch down the dough and incorporate the citrus zest and the sultanas (squeezed to remove most of the grappa). Press the dough into the cake tin and leave to rise a second time until it has doubled again in volume. Meanwhile preheat the oven to 160°C/325°F/Gas 3.

Brush the top of the loaf with beaten egg yolk and bake for 45 minutes to 1 hour. The bread is done when it makes a hollow sound when tapped, and when a knife inserted into the centre of the loaf comes out clean.

Use as below, but even better, slice, toast and butter for breakfast.

Torta di Pignoli
Pine-nut Cake

Years ago I stole a recipe from Alice Waters at Chez Panisse in Berkeley, California. It was for a rich cake which used olive oil instead of butter, and was flavoured with a sweet dessert wine. Reception of this dish in Britain was guardedly polite, i.e. they hated it, but the Italians went berserk about it. Over the years it has mutated slightly and acquired a topping of pine nuts and icing sugar. Serve it with Baked Plums (see page 180), or fresh fruit salad and mascarpone.

10 people
4 tbsp top-quality olive oil
125 g plain flour
4 x size 3 eggs
125 g caster sugar
1 tsp equal parts finely grated lemon
    and orange zest
2 tbsp sweet dessert wine
80 g pine nuts
icing sugar to dust

You will need a 30 cm spring-clip cake tin, and a 30 cm circle of non-stick baking paper. Preheat the oven to 150°C/300°F/Gas 2.

The best way of making this cake is with a mixer; to attempt to do it by hand is brave but foolhardy. Brush the sides of the tin with extra olive oil and dust with extra flour, shaking off the excess. Oil the base of the tin lightly and fit the circle of paper. Assemble all the ingredients: everything must be to hand, or a disaster will ensue.

Put the eggs and sugar in your mixer bowl and beat on high speed until pale, fluffy and very stiff – they should have at least doubled in volume. Add the orange and lemon zest. Turn the mixer to low and pour in the flour in a steady stream: it will combine almost immediately. Very quickly add the wine and oil, and switch off. Working even more quickly, gently mix the oil and wine into the cake batter. You do this by turning over and folding the mixture with a large spoon, while you turn the bowl by hand. Three or four folds will do.

Still at a frantic pace, pour and scrape this mixture into your prepared cake tin, and run this to your preheated oven. Shut in the oven and do not look at it or otherwise open the door for 25 minutes. When this time has elapsed peer quickly in: if the cake is rising and overbrowning, turn the oven down to 140°C/275°F/Gas 1. If it is golden and only slightly domed, leave for 5 minutes. Then more than quickly scatter with the pine nuts, dust copiously with icing sugar and return to the oven for 15 minutes or so until the cake is done and the pine nuts have started to brown. A clean knife inserted into the centre of the cake should come out very slightly moist. Allow the cake to cool on a rack in its tin for 15 minutes then remove.

Tiramisù

The Black Forest Gâteau for the 1990s, naffer than naff, yet somehow delicious. I make ridiculously complicated ones in my restaurants, but this is much simpler, and generally a huge success with the guests in Italy. The name means 'pick-me-up'.

8–10 people
4 eggs
8 tbsp caster sugar
750 g mascarpone cheese
1 wine glass Marsala wine
1 wine glass Scotch whisky
600 ml strong sweetened coffee
   (the only good use for the
   instant espresso)
2 packets sponge fingers (Italian
   are best)
unsweetened cocoa powder
good-quality dark chocolate

Combine the eggs and sugar, and beat with an electric hand whisk until stiff and white. By hand, incorporate the mascarpone, a spoonful at a time, by folding it in. Add the glass of Marsala, and whisk in quickly, trying all the time not to lose the volume of the beaten eggs and sugar. Add the whisky to the sweetened coffee and pour into a tray. Briefly dip the biscuits into this mixture, making sure they don't get saturated, and arrange in a radial pattern in the bottom of a 25 cm spring-clip tin, cutting wedges off the biscuits to fill the gaps. Spoon over half the mascarpone mix, lightly dust with cocoa, and repeat the layers of sponge fingers, mascarpone and cocoa. Grate a fine layer of good-quality dark chocolate over the finished pudding.

Chill for a minimum of 6 hours or, even better, overnight. When ready to serve, run a knife round the rim of the cake tin, pop the spring and pray.

Cantuccini
Double-baked Dry Almond Biscuits

These little almond biscuits are inestimably better than shop bought. The recipe comes from Sophie Braimbridge, a frequent guest chef at La Cacciata.

Makes 2 dozen biscuits
250 g plain flour
250 g caster sugar
1/2 tsp baking powder
1/2 tsp vanilla extract
2 x size 3 eggs, at room
   temperature
1 egg yolk
100 g almonds and hazelnuts,
   toasted and coarsely chopped
1 tsp whole aniseed
egg wash (egg yolk and water),
   to glaze

Preheat the oven to 180°C/350°F/Gas 4.

Put the flour, sugar, baking powder, vanilla, eggs and egg yolk into a food processor and blend until it forms a ball. This might take some time, but be patient. Place on a lightly floured surface and knead in the nuts and aniseed. Divide the paste in two, and roll out into log shapes, about 4 cm wide. Put on a baking tray covered with baking parchment. Keep them at least 5 cm apart as they spread while cooking. Lightly glaze with a little egg wash. Bake for about 35 minutes. Remove from the oven and reduce the temperature of the oven to 150°C/300°F/Gas 2. Cut the logs diagonally into 2.5 cm slices and lay them cut side up on the sheet. Return them to the oven for another hour, or until they are no longer soft. Cool on racks.

Torta di Cioccolata
Chocolate Torte

A rich chocolate cake, originally shown to me by Sophie Braimbridge, with definite antecedents from Chez Panisse and the River Cafe. I've adapted it slightly, and served it in Frith Street where it was described as an Italian Chocolate Brownie.

8 people

150 g whole blanched almonds
1 x 2 cm slice Panettone (see
    page 174)
165 g unsalted butter
300 g good-quality dark chocolate
150 g caster sugar
4 eggs
1/2 vanilla pod
150 g mascarpone cheese

Preheat the oven to 180°C/350°F/Gas 4.

Combine the almonds and panettone in a food processor and whizz until it forms a fine meal. Rub an 18 cm spring-clip cake tin generously with 15 g of the butter, and sprinkle with some of this mixture. Roll the mixture around to form an even coating, and then invert the cake tin to shake out excess nuts and breadcrumbs.

Melt the chocolate with 2 tbsp water in a double boiler or microwave. Whilst this is melting, cream the remaining butter and the sugar in the food processor. Add the eggs, the scraped-out vanilla seeds, chocolate, remaining nut and panettone mix and the mascarpone. Whizz until just incorporated, no more. Pour and scrape into the prepared cake tin, and bake for about 40 minutes. The cake should be just about set: cracks will appear about 2 cm in from the rim and when they have spread all around the cake in a circle, this is a pretty certain indication it is done.

Remove from the oven and leave to sit for 20 minutes before unmoulding. It is best served warm when it may be a little runny in the middle. This is not a problem; remember how much you liked raw cake mix as a kid – fight with your siblings over the bowl!

Prugne al Forno
Baked Plums

A huge variety of plums come into season in Italy during July. The commercially grown ones are scarcely any better than those available in Britain, indeed are often the same plums from the same cooperatives of growers. The less perfect looking but marvellously flavoursome home-grown plums available from the 'contadine' (literally small-holding peasant women) in Orvieto market are another matter altogether.

Cooking plums is difficult, as they often turn incredibly sour or disintegrate, frequently both. This method of baking them with an almost obscene amount of sugar avoids both problems. The plums are sweetened and the juices, comprising water from the fruit and sugar, are soured. This osmotic process achieves an exact balance of sugar, and partially preserves the fruit, so it is best to do quite a quantity. You will need a non-reactive baking dish (pyrex, enamelled metal or pottery), as the extreme acidity of the plums will attack most metals, causing discoloration and a suspect taste.

10 people

1.5 kg plums (not small ones like Mirabelles)
750 g caster sugar

Preheat the oven to 150°C/300°F/Gas 2.

Slice each plum in half along the seam, being careful to cut to the stone. Wrench gently apart and remove the stone. Put the fruit in a large bowl. When they are all prepared add the sugar and mix thoroughly.

Arrange the plum halves in your selected baking dish, stacking them on their sides, propping each other up. Add any sugar remaining in the bowl. Cut some greaseproof paper to fit inside the baking dish and cover the plums. Your baking dish must be big enough to hold the fruit in one layer. Bake in the oven for 45 minutes. Do not touch, shake or stir. Remove from the oven and set aside to cool. Be careful; the sugary juices are above boiling point and will redefine pain if slopped on to your hand. It is very important that you do not try to do anything to the plums until they are cold or they will break up, indeed they are better left in their baking dish and served from this.

Serve with an almond tart or Pine-nut Cake (see pages 168 and 176) and whipped cream. If you want, a blob of mascarpone would provide an even richer alternative to cream.

Insalata d'Arancia Zuccherata
Caramelised Orange Salad

The old standby of Italian dessert trolleys in mediocre trattorie around Britain, oranges in their caramelised juices with zest. This version uses blood oranges from Sicily (available from February to April), and slices the oranges up. Be careful when reducing the syrup to make the caramel, as sugar burns at 420°C (higher than the melting point of tin, for example), and will certainly hurt if you splash it on yourself or taste it.

6 people
8 blood oranges
250 g caster sugar
250 ml water

Mix the sugar and water in a wide stainless-steel pan and, stirring, bring to the boil. Carefully peel the skin off the oranges as thinly as you can. The best implement to use is a potato peeler. Make sure that you leave all the white pith still attached to the oranges. Finely slice the peel into thin strips and drop into the by now boiling syrup. Turn the heat down and poach this zest for 15 minutes.

Carefully sieve the syrup into a heatproof dish, then return the zest and half the syrup to the same pan and continue to cook over a medium flame until the sugar turns dark brown. Reserve the other half of the syrup and cool. This is why you are using a stainless pan, because it allows you to see exactly how brown the caramelised syrup and zest are. Do not be too timid: it must be nut brown, but on no account allow it to blacken. As soon as you are satisfied with the colour, add the other reserved half of the syrup. This will dilute the syrup, stopping it setting and cooling it down a little. Allow to cool and stir. If you don't caramelise the zesty part, the whole mixture will not be flavoured enough.

While the zest and syrup are reducing and browning, prepare the oranges. Cut the top and bottom off each orange and then with a small sharp knife slice the pith off in vertical strips, leaving a fully peeled orange. This sounds difficult but isn't. Slice the peeled oranges into rounds and arrange in a serving dish or bowl. Pick out any pips you can easily remove. Set aside until the zest and caramel syrup is only warm and then pour this on to the orange slices. Carefully turn the slices in this liquid until coated. Make sure the zest is evenly distributed.

Best served on the same day.

Budino di Riso al Latte
Venetian Rice Pudding

The sultanas and pine nuts in this dish indicate a Middle Eastern influence. Venice, where this dish is almost an obsession, was the first Christian state to trade with the Ottoman Empire, continuing centuries of lucratively being the gateway to western Europe for spices, sugar, dye and other expensive exotica. This bears a clear resemblance to British rice pudding and to a similar dish served in Bruges (Bruges and Venice were trading partners, the former the principal outlet for Venetian trade in our neck of the woods). Venice as a trading centre has declined since the fifteenth century, but its culinary glories are largely intact.

This dish ideally should use carnaroli rice if you can find it, otherwise substitute arborio or at a real pinch Patna.

6–8 people
200 g rice (see above)
1 litre milk
500 ml double cream
1 vanilla pod
130 g sultanas
a little brandy or grappa
100 g caster sugar
a pinch of salt
a little powdered cinnamon
a little grated nutmeg
100 g pine nuts, toasted lightly
grated zest of 1 lemon
a little butter

You can prepare this dish a day ahead and either serve cold or reheat in individual buttered moulds.

Put the milk in a trustworthy pan and bring to a slow boil over a low flame. While this is happening carefully split the vanilla pod lengthways and with the tip of the knife scrape the seeds out. Whisk these into the heating milk and add the emptied pod. Put the sultanas to soak in the brandy or grappa.

When the milk reaches boiling, add the cream and the rice then turn the flame up to medium. Cook, stirring almost continuously, for 20 minutes. Then add the sugar, a pinch of salt, the cinnamon and the nutmeg. Turn the heat down to low, then stir and cook slowly, stirring occasionally, for a further 20 minutes.

Now add the pine nuts, the soaked sultanas and the grated zest of the lemon. Mix thoroughly and allow to cool off the heat. If not using soon transfer to a container and refrigerate.

Preheat the oven to its maximum.

To serve, transfer to a buttered gratin dish and bake until browning, bubbling and rising – about 20 minutes.

Delicious as this rice is, it needs something more (like the spoon of jam in English rice pudding). My favourite would be the Caramelised Orange Salad overleaf.

GELATO | ICE CREAM

Walk into any gelateria in Italy and you will be presented with a bewildering array of delicious home-made ice creams and sorbets, all made on the premises, all surely so much better than anywhere else. This is a myth: the choice is dispiritingly universal across the country. 'Home-made' in that industrially produced mixes and syrups are processed on the premises in sleek machines (they are, after all, Italian machines), which incorporate as much air into the product as possible. 'Delicious', no, rather dull, and 'better than anywhere else', simply not true: Moscow has and has always had better ice cream. There are very good gelaterie, usually one in every city, and the queues of Italians in it will announce the fact, but even these produce an ice that is not to the same standard as the best of other countries. Here I give the basic ice cream recipes. They are unashamedly not Italian but are easily achievable without an ice-cream machine.

Gelato al Caramello
Caramel Ice Cream

This recipe is made at La Cacciata nearly every Wednesday morning for serving after the pizze that evening. Sarah Robson, my partner at the school, seems particularly fond of it!

10–12 people
1 litre milk (not skimmed, sterilised or
    anythinged, ordinary milk!)
8 egg yolks
230 g caster sugar
a few drops of vanilla essence
500 ml double cream

Scald the milk, i.e. heat it until nearly boiling. Whisk the egg yolks with 80 g of the sugar by hand in a heavy saucepan until just combined, then pour in the hot milk, whisking all the while. Heat to 80°C/176°F, or until it thickens enough to coat the back of a metal spoon. Add the vanilla essence, and allow to cool, stirring.

Use a stainless-steel, aluminium or pale enamelled wide pan: the reason for this is that it will allow you to judge the degree of brownness in the melting sugar. Dark pans hide the colour, and the tendency would be to undercook the sugar, resulting in toffee, not caramel. Melt the remaining 150 g sugar over a medium heat. Do not stir, swirl the pan instead (if you stir, half the sugar will cling to the spoon). Take the sugar to dark brown (not tan, not café au lait but dark brown). Remove from the heat and rather gingerly pour in the double cream. It will splutter and spit for a few seconds. Stir and return to a low heat until all the lumps of caramel that formed on contact with the cold cream dissolve into it. You have just made a butterscotch sauce.

Combine the ice cream mixture and the caramel cream mixture, then freeze in the same manner as the Vanilla Ice Cream opposite.

Gelato alla Vaniglia
Vanilla Ice Cream

To my mind the best of all ice creams, when made properly. There is a purity about it that forbids tampering.

10–12 people
2 vanilla pods
6 egg yolks
175 g caster sugar
500 ml full cream milk
500 ml double cream

Split the vanilla pods longitudinally and using the point of a small knife scrape out the seeds on to a white saucer. Put these seeds into a mixing bowl with the egg yolks and sugar, then whisk just enough to amalgamate.

While you are doing this, scald the milk with the empty vanilla pod in a medium-sized trustworthy saucepan (i.e. one that will not scorch – enamelled ones are particularly bad for this. Scalding means heating the milk to just below boiling point). Pour the scalded milk and pods over the sugar and eggs and mix thoroughly then return to the milk pan. Put the mixture back on a medium heat and cook, stirring continuously, until it achieves 80°C/176°F or a coating consistency (when the mixture coats the back of a metal spoon). Do not overcook this, or it will be milky scrambled eggs. For ice creams this custard mix does not need cooking except for health reasons – heating to 80°C/176°F ensures the demise of nasty bacteria. As soon as the desired consistency or temperature is reached, pour in the double cream, remove from the heat and stir, then leave to cool. (Retrieve the vanilla pod, rinse, dry and use for making vanilla sugar.)

When cool, place in an ice-cream machine, and churn until done, or whatever the manufacturer recommends. If making *without* a machine, pour the finished mixture into a strong plastic bowl. The bowl should firstly fit your freezer and secondly be no more than half full. When nearly cold put in your freezer for 30 minutes. Remove and stir with a hand whisk until smooth. Return to the freezer and give a further 15 minutes, then whisk again. Repeat until the mixture becomes thick and difficult to whisk. From this point on you can simply leave it in the freezer, as all the previous whisking has probably prevented too many ice crystals forming. (A few crystals are no bad thing, they show your guests it is home-made!)

185

Broths, Sauces and Relishes

Brodo di Pesce
Fish Broth

Remarkably similar to fish soup, this unthickened flavoursome broth is the base for innumerable bouillabaisse-like dishes around Italy's coastline. In this book it is essential for Minestrone di Razza (see page 56).

Makes about 2 litres

1 hen crab, about 1 kg (ask your fishmonger to
   kill it and chop it)
4 kg bones and heads of non-oily fish, gills
   removed and thoroughly rinsed
good olive oil
2 celery sticks, coarsely diced
2 onions, peeled and coarsely diced
1 fennel bulb, coarsely diced
2 carrots, peeled and coarsely diced
1 leek, diced and rinsed
1 large piece orange zest
1 large piece lemon zest
1 large red chilli
4 garlic cloves, peeled and minced
2 bay leaves
a handful of parsley stalks
500 g tinned tomato pieces
1 bottle dry white wine
a little Pernod or anisette
a tiny pinch of powdered saffron
salt and pepper

In a large (very large) pan heat 6 tbsp olive oil, and add the celery, onion, fennel, carrot, leek and zests. Over a brisk heat sweat these until they start to colour, then add the chilli, garlic, bay leaves and parsley stalks. Toss and then add the tomato and wine. Stir and bring this lot to the boil. Throw in the crab bits and the fish bones and heads, stir and then add enough water to barely cover the bones.

Cook this concoction at a medium simmer, stirring and skimming occasionally, for 1 hour. Allow to cool and then tip into another receptacle through a colander. Allow the debris in the colander to drain thoroughly, pressing on it with the back of a ladle. When you are sure you have extracted all of the juices, discard the debris. Wrap in several plastic bags as it soon gets pongy.

Put the broth through a fine sieve, again pressing to extract all the liquid, and return to the boil in a clean pan. Skim thoroughly then add the Pernod and saffron, and simmer for an hour until the liquid has reduced by half. Taste and adjust the seasoning.

The reason for extracting all the solids is to prevent them going rancid, which they quickly do. The cloudy but tasty broth can now be frozen if you wish.

Brodo di Pollo
Chicken Broth

A two-stage recipe. Firstly it's a simple, relatively quick chicken stock then, if you wish, you can poach a chicken in it to give both a main course and a good chicken soup. The chicken used in the stock is part bouillon and part browned chicken wings.

Makes about 2 litres

1.5 kg chicken wings
2 carrots, peeled and coarsely chopped
2 onions, peeled and coarsely chopped
1 head celery, chopped and then washed
2 bay leaves, 1 sprig thyme, 1 sprig rosemary, a
   few parsley stalks, tied into a bouquet garni
6 chicken bouillon cubes (Knorr for preference)
4 litres water
1/2 bottle white wine

First trim the chicken wings. Open one out and you will see three sections: the wing tip, the middle joint and what appears to be a miniature drumstick. Separate at each joint. Scissors are very good for this but be careful, the pressure you exert on cutting the bones will do an equally effective job on your finger tips.

Put the chopped wings, vegetables and bouquet garni in a stock pot. Add the bouillon cubes and water and bring to the boil. Turn down as soon as it is boiling and add the wine. Stir and skim, and continue to cook at the barest simmer for 3 hours, skimming often.

The wings will give out a surprising amount of fat. Sieve the stock, discarding all the solids, and return to the cleaned-out pan, then bring to a rapid boil. As the stock comes to the boil it will start to form a splendid scum. You must get this off with a ladle, because if it boils in, the stock will be cloudy and taste fatty. After the first skim, add 500 ml cold water, bring back to the boil and skim again. This addition of cold water precipitates more fat and more particles to the top of the stock. Continue to boil the stock over a maximum flame, skimming regularly until it is reduced by half. Allow to cool and refrigerate or freeze.

For Poached Chicken and Chicken Soup

Use 1 large free-range chicken approximately 2 kg in weight. Follow the recipe for chicken stock up to 'continue to cook at the barest simmer for 3 hours, skimming often'. After you have done this, plunge the bird into the unsieved stock and turn the heat up to medium. As soon as it nears the boil, turn to low again, skim and simmer gently for 45 minutes. You may need to add more water to cover the chicken, and also to use a drop lid to hold the rather buoyant bird under the liquid's surface. After 45 minutes (an hour in all actually, since after you put the bird in, it took about 15 minutes to return to the boil), skim one more time, take off the heat and allow the chicken to cool in its stock. By the time the stock is cold the chicken will be perfectly cooked, moist and tender.

Remove the chicken from the stock with a spider, wrap and refrigerate. Sieve the stock as in the previous recipe, skim, degrease and reduce in the same manner. You must do this very thoroughly if you want a good clear soup.

The resulting soup can be reheated with freshly prepared diced leek, carrot, onion and celery boiled in it, and a final addition of the gently heated, sliced poached chicken breast. Another use is as a clear chicken soup with noodles: any of Italy's amazing range of soup pasta will do.

The best use for the poached chicken apart from in its own broth is Insalata di Cappone (see page 141).

Brodo di Verdura
Vegetable Broth

At various points in the book, vegetable broths are used as a base for pasta sauces, minestrone etc. Each of them varies slightly – asparagus stock for asparagus risotto, pea stock for Risi e Bisi – but this is a good basic recipe and technique.

Makes about 2 litres

2 onions, peeled and coarsely chopped
2 large carrots, peeled and coarsely chopped
2 celery sticks, peeled and coarsely chopped
2 leeks, chopped and washed thoroughly
1 small handful parsley stalks, 2 bay leaves,
    1 sprig rosemary, 1 sprig thyme, tied into a
    bouquet garni
2 tbsp groundnut oil
salt and pepper

Place all the vegetables and the bouquet garni in a large pan with the oil. Over a medium heat cook for 10 minutes (sweating) until the vegetables are very lightly coloured, glistening, and the onions have gone translucent. Season with salt and pepper and cover with 4 litres water. Bring to the boil over a high heat, skim, turn down to medium, and cook for 1 hour at a rapid simmer. Allow to cool, sieve and return to the cleaned-out pan. Boil vigorously until reduced by half. Place all the vegetables and the bouquet garni in a large pan with the oil. Over a medium heat cook for 10 minutes (sweating) until the vegetables are very lightly coloured, glistening, and the onions have gone translucent. Season with salt and pepper and cover with 4 litres of water. Bring to the boil over a high heat, skim, turn down to medium, and cook for 1 hour at a rapid simmer. Allow to cool, sieve and return to the cleaned-out pan. Boil vigorously until reduced by half.

Infused Oil

This oil, easily made and virtually eternal if stored in the fridge, keeps cropping up throughout the book. You may become addicted to it.

500 ml good olive oil
12 small dried chillies, rehydrated by soaking in
    warm water for 10 minutes, dried and
chopped
2 bay leaves
2 lime leaves (optional)
1 sprig fresh rosemary
4 garlic cloves, peeled and roughly sliced

Heat all the ingredients over a very low heat for half an hour. Allow to cool and bottle. Keep in the fridge when not needed.

Rouille

This is a totally ersatz rouille, but I like it, so if you wish to sneer go and look up some incredibly tiresome, utterly authentic recipe for yourself. Serve with the Skate Minestrone on page 56.

1 egg
2 tbsp harissa (hot North African chilli paste)
2 garlic cloves, peeled
juice of 1/2 lemon
2 tbsp tomato ketchup

1 small tin anchovies, drained
a little parsley
approx. 300 ml good olive oil

Blend everything except for the oil in a food processor. With the machine running, add the oil gradually. Keep pouring and blending until nice and thick. It may take more oil than specified.

Pesto

Never ever dream of making this in a mortar and pestle. It's incredibly tedious, and to my mind only succeeds in over-oxidising the basil, turning it an unattractive khaki colour. The quantity made here requires an enormous amount of basil, and I recommend you make it in summer when it is relatively cheap. You will also need a couple of clean screw-top jars to keep it in. The best way of sterilising a jar these days is to run it through a dishwasher at high heat.

enough basil leaves to fill your food processor
    loosely
100 g pine nuts
150 g Parmesan, grated
4 garlic cloves, peeled
salt and pepper
very good olive oil

Combine the pine nuts, Parmesan and garlic in the food processor, and chop to a coarse meal. Season with salt and pepper. Fill the food processor with the basil, chop for a few seconds, then remove the lid and stir the ingredients. Replace the lid and continue chopping. Pour in enough olive oil to form a stiff paste. Taste for seasoning. It may need more olive oil. I cannot give a precise quantity of olive oil, but it's probably in the region of 300 ml.

Working quite quickly, as the mixture tends to discolour rapidly – at the moment it will be a bright green and filling your kitchen with the wonderful scent of summer – pack into your prepared jars. Tap the jars lightly when full on a folded teatowel; this will drive any bubbles of air to the top. Using a rubber spatula or the back of a clean spoon, press the pesto surface flat. Pour in enough olive oil to cover it completely. Seal the jars and refrigerate until needed.

The pesto will keep unopened for a considerable time in your fridge. Once you open it, you only have 2–3 days. Remember each time you use it to smooth down the surface and re-oil. This will prolong its shelf life.

Should you be lucky enough to find aged Pecorino (a sheep's milk cheese), it can be substituted for Parmesan, making the whole thing much more authentic.

Salsa Verde
Green Sauce

There are innumerable recipes for this basic Italian relish. They all have parsley, garlic and oil in common. This is one of the more complicated ones, and was taken from Claudia Roden's *The Food of Italy*.

Of the herbs, at least half should be flat-leaf parsley; the other herbs can vary according to availability, but must include mint and basil. A small amount of tarragon is an interesting addition.

enough mixed herbs to fill your food processor
    loosely (see overleaf)
6 garlic cloves, peeled
very good olive oil, approx. 400 ml

Chop the garlic first in the food processor, add the herbs and chop a little, then add the olive oil in a stream until a thick green sauce results.

Optional Additions

1. 1 tbsp rinsed capers with 1 tbsp good-quality red wine vinegar. This makes a sharper sauce rather akin to an Italian mint sauce, and is usually served with boiled meats.
2. 3 heaped tbsp mostarda di frutta added to the basic recipe. Remember to remove any stones from the fruit, otherwise you will have an unpleasant task looking for them as they rattle around in the food processor. This relish is particularly excellent as an accompaniment to cotechino and lentils.

Salsa alla Besciamella
Béchamel Sauce

This is only used once in the book, but it is a good general recipe for a sauce that has gone out of fashion and which I find delicious. The Italians have excellent pre-made béchamel in little cardboard cartons. These have a limited availability in Britain, but I recommend you to try them if you see them.

1 litre milk
1 bay leaf
1 small onion, peeled and studded with 6 cloves
50 g butter

50 g plain flour
salt and pepper
freshly grated nutmeg

Slowly bring the milk to the boil with the bay leaf and the onion. Slowly, because we wish to infuse the milk with the bay and onion flavours.

Melt the butter in another pan (it must be big enough to comfortably hold the milk), then add the flour. Stir in to make a roux by cooking over a medium heat, stirring continuously with a wooden spoon for 10 minutes. Slowly start to add the strained milk. Stir well to avoid lumps. When all the milk has been added, and has been absorbed by the flour, cook for 20 minutes until thick and creamy. Season to taste with salt, pepper and nutmeg, and use immediately. If not using immediately, pour into a bowl and press a sheet of clingfilm on to the surface of the sauce before it forms a skin. Allow to cool and refrigerate.

Salsa di Pomodoro
Tomato Sauce

There is no point in cooking a tomato sauce with fresh tomatoes in Britain. The fruit will simply never have enough flavour and the sauce will be acidic, thin and generally not sexy. Plum tomatoes are properly ripened in sun-drenched lands and then put in tins, use them. Having said that, the Italians have been using Britain and America as a dumping ground for very inferior brands of tinned tomatoes for a long time. This is now changing and many good brands are available including the supermarkets' own ones. I tend to use the tinned chopped tomatoes (pezzi di pomodori) as my sauce material (geddit?). This sauce is ridiculously quick and simple, no onion, no celery, no sweating of ingredients: simply simmer tinned tomato pieces with flavourings until they reach the right consistency.

In a stainless pan simmer 1 kg of tinned tomato pieces in their liquid with salt, pepper and a little sugar, 4 tbsp good olive oil, 1 minced garlic clove, and 4 basil leaves.

Sauce 1
Simmer for a few minutes. This is now suitable for pizze.

Sauce 2
Simmer for about half an hour until it has reduced and concentrated by about one-third. A good general-purpose tomato sauce.

Sauce 3
Slowly simmer and concentrate. Reduce it by 75 per cent and use it sparingly as a relish or when a recipe calls for a rich sauce.

Sauce 4
'Arrabiata' – internally angry or irritated. This is basically Sauce 2 with the addition of hot chillies to taste. Serve with penne or fusilli – no Parmesan.

Sauce 5
As for Sauce 2, with the addition of chopped good anchovies and stoned black olives at the end of the cooking process, it becomes 'Napoletana'.

Crisp Breadcrumbs

A perennial problem at my restaurants revolves around leftover croûtons (crostini), which we serve with fish soup. They simple aren't good enough the next day, so I pulverise them in a food processor to produce olive-oil crumbs.

Make crostini according to the recipe on page 102, then when cool (or leftover), whirl briefly in a food processor. Spread out on a baking sheet and sprinkle with a little olive oil and re-bake in a slow oven (140°C/275°F/Gas 1) until golden and crisp. Allow to cool again, then season and whirl again briefly until an even crumb is produced. Do not reduce to a powder.

Various flavourings can be added to these crumbs (pesto, for instance).

INDEX